国家汉办/孔子学院总部
Hanban/Confucius Institute Headquarters

Emperor Qin Shihuang

Collection of Critical Biographies of Chinese Thinkers

(Concise Edition, Chinese-English)

Editors-in-chief: Zhou Xian, Cheng Aimin

Author: Tong Qiang　Li Xiyan
Translator: Wang Zhengwen
Expert: Jin Jing

Nanjing University Press

《中国思想家评传》简明读本 － 中英文版 －
主 编 周 宪 程爱民

秦始皇

著 者／童 强　　李喜燕
Tong Qiang　Li Xiyan
译 者／王正文 Wang Zhengwen
审 校／Eric Harrison Paul
审 读／金 晶 Jin Jing

南京大学出版社

Editors: Li Haixia, Wang Yuyao
Cover designed by Zhao Qin

First published 2010
by Nanjing University Press
No. 22, Hankou Road, Nanjing City, 210093
www.NjupCo.com

Chinese Library Cataloguing in Publication Data
The CIP data for this title is on file with the Chinese Library.

ISBN10: 7-305-06608-5(pbk)
ISBN13: 978-7-305-06608-5(pbk)

《中国思想家评传》简明读本（中英文版）

编 委 会

Books available in the collection

Confucius
《孔子》
978-7-305-06611-5

Laozi
《老子》
978-7-305-06607-8

Emperor Qin Shihuang
《秦始皇》
978-7-305-06608-5

Li Bai
《李白》
978-7-305-06609-2

Cao Xueqin
《曹雪芹》
978-7-305-06610-8

Du Fu
《杜甫》
978-7-305-06826-3

Zhuangzi
《庄子》
978-7-305-07177-5

Sima Qian
《司马迁》
978-7-305-07294-9

Mencius
《孟子》
978-7-305-07583-4

Mozi
《墨子》
978-7-305-07970-2

总序

General Preface

China is one of the cradles of world civilization, enjoying over five thousand years of history. It has produced many outstanding figures in the history of ancient thought, and left a rich philosophical heritage for both the Chinese people and the entire humanity. The fruit of these thinkers was to establish unique schools that over the long course of history have been continuously interpreted and developed. Today much of these thoughts are as relevant as ever and of extreme vitality for both China and the rest of the world. For instance, the ideal of "humaneness" and the concept of "harmony" taught by Confucius, the founder of Confucianism, have been venerated without ceasing by contemporary China as well as other Asian nations.

Ancient Chinese dynasties came and went, with each new dynasty producing its own scintillating system of thought. These rare and beautiful flowers of philosophy are grounded in the hundred schools vying for attention in pre-Qin times and the broad yet deep classical scholarship of Han and Tang times and in the simple yet profound occult learning of the Wei and Jin dynasties together with the entirely rational learning of Song and Ming Neo-Confucianism. The fertile soil of religious belief was Buddhism's escape from the emptiness of the sensual world and Daoism's spiritual cultivation in the search for identification with the immortals. The founders of these systems of thought included teachers, scholars, poets, politicians, scientists and monks— they made great contributions to such disparate cultural fields in ancient China as philosophy, politics, military science, economics, law, handicrafts, science and technology, literature, art, and religion. The ancient Chinese venerated them for their wisdom and for following moral paths, and called them sages, worthies, saints, wise men, and great masters, etc. Their words and writings, and sometimes their life experiences, constitute the rich matter of ancient Chinese thought distilled by later generations. The accomplishments of Chinese thought are rich and varied, and permeate such spiritual traditions as the harmony between humans and nature, the unification of thought and action, and the need for calmness during vigorous action, synthesizing the old and innovating something new.

Nanjing University Press has persisted over the last twenty years in publishing the 200-book series, *Collection of Critical Biographies of Chinese Thinkers*, under the general editorship of Professor Kuang Yaming, late honorary president of Nanjing University. This collection is the largest-scale project of research on Chinese thinking and culture undertaken since the beginning of the twentieth century. It selected more than 270 outstanding figures from Chinese history, composed their biographies and criticized their

中国是世界文明的发源地之一，有五千多年的文明史。在中国古代思想史上，涌现出了许许多多杰出的思想家，为中华民族乃至整个人类留下了丰富的思想遗产。这些思想成果独树一帜，在漫长的历史中又不断地被阐释、被发展，很多思想对于今天的中国乃至世界而言，仍然历久弥新，极具生命力。比如，儒家学派创始人孔子"仁"的理念、"和"的思想，不仅在当代中国，在其他亚洲国家也一直备受推崇。

古代中国朝代更迭，每一个朝代都有灿烂夺目的思想文化。百家争鸣的先秦诸子、博大宏深的汉唐经学、简易幽远的魏晋玄学、尽心知性的宋明理学是思想学术的奇葩；佛教的色空禅悦、道教的神仙修养是宗教信仰的沃土；其他如经世济民的政治、经济理想，巧夺天工的科技、工艺之道，风雅传神、丹青不老的文学艺术……都蕴涵着丰富的思想。这些思想的创造者中有教师、学者、诗人、政治家、科学家、僧人……他们在中国古代的哲学、政治、军事、经济、法律、工艺、科技、文学、艺术、宗教等各个文明领域内贡献巨大。古代中国人尊敬那些充满智慧、追求道德的人，称呼他们为圣人、贤人、哲人、智者、大师等，他们的言论、著作或被后人总结出来的经验构成了中国古代思想的重要内容，在丰富多彩中贯穿着天人合一、知行合一、刚健中和等精神传统，表现出综合创新的特色。

南京大学出版社坚持20余年，出版了由南京大学已故名誉校长匡亚明教授主编的《中国思想家评传丛书》，这套丛书共200部，是中国20世纪以来最为宏大的中国传统思想文化研究工程，选出了中国历史上270余位杰出人物，为他们写传记，

intellectual accomplishments; all in all, it is a rigorous and refined academic work. On this foundation, we introduce this series of concise readers, which provides much material in a simple format. It includes the cream of the crop of great figures relatively familiar to foreign readers. We have done our best to use plain but vivid language to narrate their human stories of interest; this will convey the wisdom of their thought and display the cultural magnificence of the Chinese people. In the course of spiritually communing with these representative thinkers from ancient China, readers will certainly be able to apprehend the undying essence of thoughts of the Chinese people.

Finally, we are deeply grateful for the support from Hanban/ Confucius Institute Headquarters, and the experts from home and abroad for their joint efforts in writing and translating this series.

Editors
November, 2009

评论他们的思想成就，是严肃精深的学术著作。在此基础上推出的这套简明读本，则厚积薄发，精选出国外读者相对较为熟悉的伟大人物，力求用简洁生动的语言，通过讲述有趣的人物故事，传达他们的思想智慧，展示中华民族绚烂多姿的文化。读者在和这些中国古代有代表性的思想家的心灵对话中，一定能领略中华民族思想文化生生不息的精髓。

最后，我们衷心感谢国家汉办/孔子学院总部对本项目提供了巨大的支持，感谢所有参与此套丛书撰写和翻译工作的中外专家学者为此套丛书所做的辛勤而卓有成效的工作。

编者

2009年11月

目录
Contents

一 引言

Chapter I Introduction

Over 2 200 years ago, a great empire arose in the vast land of China.

It was the Qin Dynasty.The self-proclaimed First Emperor of the Qin Dynasty (named Ying Zheng) was one of the greatest monarchs in ancient China. Within 10 years, he annexed the other six states—Qi, Chu, Yan, Zhao, Han and Wei—and in 221 B.C., brought to an end the country's splitting polity which had lasted for several hundred years. For the first time in history, China was united under one ruler.

The territory of this empire was immense: It extended eastward to the Bohai Sea and Yellow Sea; it went westward as far as to the provinces of Gansu and Ningxia; its southern boundary began in the South China Sea and ended at the Great Wall in the north. This territory roughly demarcated the core areas of the domain of China. From that time on, the Chinese people have taken for granted that this vast land is a unified country. This idea comes in large measure from Qin Shihuang's original unification of China.

Once established, this nascent empire began to carry out bold and resolute reforms by promoting a strong central government and setting up a complete system of governance. Within this system, the emperor stood at the top, with three high-ranked officials and nine ministers under him. The central government abolished the hereditary vassal system and established the "Jun-Xian System," namely, a system of prefectures and counties ruled directly by the imperial government. In economic matters, the emperor standardized weights and measures, as well as the currency. The emperor also ardently advocated the uniformity of thinking and ethics as a central theme of national ideology. The judiciary system constituted uniform laws and regulations, and emphasized running state affairs according to law and strict law enforcement. Culturally speaking, the new administration standardized the Chinese written language, which promoted the formation of a unified Chinese identity and culture that extended throughout the empire.

Under the emperor's personal supervision, many Herculean projects were undertaken, such as the Zheng Guo Canal, the Lingqu Canal, a vast network of roads, the Great Wall (which is the focus of world attention even today), the palace buildings in Xianyang (e.g., the Epang Palace), and the city-sized mausoleum on the mountain called Lishan Mountain (including the life-sized terracotta warriors). Not only were these projects monumental at the time, but some, such as the Great Wall, are considered wonders of the world even today. These ambitious projects not only symbolized imperial power, but to some degree also contributed to the empire's actual emerging prowess.

To ensure his supreme power, Emperor Qin Shihuang held a grand

距今两千两百多年前，在中国这片辽阔的土地上，一个帝国诞生了。

这就是秦王朝。它的君主姓嬴（yíng），名政，自称始皇帝，是中国古代伟大的帝王之一。他用了短短十年的时间，终于在公元前221年，吞并了其他六个诸侯国——齐、楚、燕、赵、韩、魏，结束了战国以来数百年分裂割据的政治局面，实现了中国历史上第一次真正意义的统一。

这是一个疆域辽阔的帝国：东到渤海、黄海，西至甘肃、宁夏，南起南海，北抵长城，初步划定了中国版图的核心区域。此后，中国人一直都把这片广阔土地上统一的国家形态视为理所当然，这不能不说与秦始皇最初统一中国有关。

新兴的帝国随之进行大刀阔斧的改革，推行中央集权制度，建立一整套完整的统治模式。在政治上，以皇权为中心，下设三公、九卿等朝廷官职，取消传统的封建制，实行郡、县两级主要行政区划；在经济上，统一度量衡和货币制度；在思想上，倡导统一的观念体系和道德规范；在司法上，制定统一的法律法规，强调依法治国，严格执法；在文化上，实行统一的书写文字，促进文化共同体和中华民族心理认同的形成。

在秦始皇亲自组织下，秦朝还兴建了大批帝国工程，郑国渠、灵渠、驰道（道路工程）、举世瞩目的万里长城、咸阳宫廷建筑（阿房宫等）和骊山陵墓（包括兵马俑）等。这些工程规模宏大，不仅在当时为世人所惊叹，就是在今天，包括长城在内的几项工程仍堪称世界奇迹。巨大的工程成为帝国权力意志的象征，甚至就是权力自身的实体。

为了威服天下，同时也为了亲身感受帝国的富饶，秦始皇

ceremony to worship Heaven atop the Mountain Tai. In addition, in order to see the beautiful and fertile land of his empire with his own eyes, the emperor made frequent inspection tours of major cities and many other places in the country. While ancient Chinese emperors were expected to build palaces and mausoleums, to hold grand ceremonies, and to tour the country, Qin Shihuang's projects were too ambitious to be deemed proper within traditional social norms. They placed great burdens upon the people, including strict laws and heavy taxes, which incited and aggravated social conflicts. Furthermore, in his late years Qin Shihuang spent extravagantly on his quest for the elixir of immortality, which only worsened his standing in the eyes of the people. In 210 B.C., the emperor died of illness while on one of his inspection tours, and his son Huhai became the emperor, known as Qin Ershi (the Second Emperor of Qin). Qin Ershi, however, was unable to improve the political situation in the empire, and only three years after the First Emperor's death, the grand edifice of the Qin Empire collapsed.

Much has changed with the passage of time, yet even today we continue to study Emperor Qin Shihuang and his great empire. He was both an influential emperor and a brutal tyrant; despite his great talents and bold vision, he also made some disastrous policy decisions. He displayed unusual wisdom in judgment in annexing the other six states, but in his latter years he indulged in the superstitious and costly pursuit of the Elixir of Life. Whereas he once commanded an invincible army, the impregnable empire this army defended was overthrown by a farmers' rebellion.

Even so, Qin Shihuang is clearly both the destroyer of an old age and the creator of a new one.

举行了祭祀天地即封禅（shàn）的重大仪式，多次巡游全国各地。在古代，天子修宫殿、筑陵墓、行封禅和巡游，均是合乎礼仪的行为，然而秦始皇的规模往往超出了传统的礼制，加重了人民的负担，严酷的刑罚和繁重的赋税激化了社会矛盾。他晚年又动用大量的财力物力寻求长生不死的仙药，更是不得人心。公元前210年，秦始皇在巡游的途中病逝。他的儿子胡亥登上王位，成为秦二世皇帝，但他根本无力改善帝国的政治。秦始皇死后不到三年的时间，秦帝国的大厦，便在顷刻之间灰飞烟灭了。

物换星移，时光流逝，直到今天，我们仍然热衷于谈论这位帝王和他的帝国：他是一位伟大的君主，可无疑又是一位暴君；他具有雄才大略，可是又有许多政策失误；他在兼并六国时表现出准确的现实判断，可是晚年却沉迷于神仙世界和长生不老之术；他的军队曾经所向无敌，然而由这支军队捍卫的固若金汤的帝国，却又在揭竿而起的农夫们的打击下一蹶（jué）不振。

毫无疑问，他既是一位旧历史的终结者，又是一位新时代的开创者。

秦始皇画像

Portrait of Emperor Qin Shihuang

二 君王的诞生

Chapter Ⅱ Birth of Emperor

It has become a rule in Chinese history that the appearance of miracles often coincides with the births of kings or emperors. But given the short-lived reign of the Qin Dynasty, there was hardly time to add any mythical color to Emperor Qin Shihuang's birth before it came to an end. Consequently, his birth seems relatively ordinary.

Qin Shihuang's father, Zichu, was one of the princes of the Qin State. During the Warring States Period, the wars between states were so frequent that in order to form an alliance, it was common practice to exchange members of the nobility between states as pledges of good faith. As such, at one time Zichu was held hostage in the Zhao State. Usually these hostages were entitled to special treatment, but if the hostages' home states violated the treaty of alliance, they faced the prospect of losing their lives.

Zichu encountered poor treatment in the state of Zhao, as the states of Qin and Zhao had frequently gone to war in the past. In 260 B.C., when Qin attacked the Han State, Han submitted itself to Zhao. For this reason, Qin declared war on Zhao. In a place called Changping, the two states' armies met in a fierce battle. The Zhao army lost more than 400 000 soldiers in the battle, and were defeated by the Qin forces. Shortly thereafter, the Qin army besieged Handan, the Zhao capital. In these circumstances, Zichu, as a hostage, was despised by the Zhao people and received no special treatment. Additionally, since his home state of Qin only gave him a meager allowance, he eked out a miserable existence.

At that time in the Wei State lived a wealthy merchant named Lü Buwei, who frequently traveled from one capital city of a state to another on business. One day in Handan Lü Buwei met the miserable Prince Zichu and felt pity for him. "This man can be hoarded as a rare commodity," Lü said to himself. He meant that a rare commodity sells well, and it is unusually worthwhile to invest in. In Zichu, Lü Buwei found a prime opportunity to make a profitable investment, as he had already predicted his own promising future.

"If I go into farming," Lü Buwei asked his father, "how much profit can I gain from it?"

"Tenfold the money you've invested," his father replied.

"What's the profit if I run a jewelry business?" "A hundredfold."

"How much profit would I gain from helping a prince become a king?"

"This investment will bring you incalculable profit," said his father.

Hearing this, Lü Buwei said, "Nowadays farming is rather toilsome and the gain can scarcely support a family. But if I can assist a king in governing a

帝王的降生总是充满神异，但秦王朝似乎还来不及为秦始皇的出生抹上一道神话色彩，帝国就崩溃了。因此，这一回，皇帝的降临显得有些普通。

秦始皇的父亲是秦国的王子，名叫子楚。起初，子楚作为秦国的人质留居在赵国。战国时期，诸侯国之间战争频繁，两国之间为了结盟，便互派王室成员作为人质抵押到对方国家。通常来说，人质在他国会受到优待，但是，一旦本国违背盟约，人质就会面临生命的危险。

子楚在赵国的境遇并不好。秦国与赵国多次交战，子楚不断受到牵连。尤其是公元前260年，秦国攻打韩国，韩国人投降了赵国，于是秦兵进攻赵国。在一个叫做长平的地方大战一场，赵军失败，有四十多万人被杀。不久，秦军又围攻赵国都城邯郸（hán dān）。在这种情形下，作为人质的子楚无疑要遭到赵人的憎恨，根本谈不上什么优厚的待遇。秦国所给的资助很少，子楚的生活非常清贫。

当时，有一位魏国的大商人吕不韦，因做生意来往于各国的都市。在邯郸，他看到了穷困落魄的子楚，非常怜惜，自言自语说："此奇货可居。"意思是说，物以稀为贵，难得的东西正可以投资经营。在子楚身上，吕不韦看到了一个可以获利无穷的投资机会，更看到了自己的远大前程。

他问父亲："耕田种地，能得到多少利润？"

父亲回答："十倍。"

"经营珠宝，能得到多少利润？"

"百倍。"

"扶助王子登上王位，能得到多少利润？"

"无数。"

吕不韦说："现在耕田种地，辛苦劳作，还不能求得温饱。

state and maintaining stability, not only I but also my offspring of many generations can benefit from it. That is exactly what I want to do."

So Lü Buwei decided to provide financial aid to Zichu and help him to take the throne of Qin. When Zichu, who was destitute at that time, heard Lü Buwei's scheme, he could hardly believe his ears. It was a scheme he could have never imagined. He made repeated bows to Lü Buwei and said eagerly, "If you can succeed in your scheme, I will share the lands of the Qin with you."

At the time, the King Zhao Xiang of Qin held the throne, and the father of Zichu was merely a crown prince, i.e. an heir apparent with a title Lord Anguo. Lord Anguo had more than 20 sons and Zichu was neither the first born nor the beloved one, therefore it was almost impossible for him to be the crown heir. However, Lord Anguo had a favorite concubine called Lady Huayang who had no children of her own, and Lü Buwei and Zichu decided to capitalize on that.

In contemporary Chinese language, the activities such as going into business, managing enterprises and producing products can be classified as "economy." But in ancient Chinese language, the activities such as ruling a state and bringing peace and stability to the state were also regarded as "economy," for commerce and politics had many things in common. Lü Buwei's success in commerce soon turned into political wisdom.

He began to provide Zichu with large sums of money, which enabled Zichu to come into contact with many influential figures in high society, allowing him to build up his reputation. At the same time, Lü Buwei went in person to Xianyang, the Qin capital, where he managed a meeting with Lady Huayang. With eloquent language, he attempted to persuade Lady Huayang into believing that Zichu was a benevolent and wise man, and that because he was a hostage in the Zhao State, he missed Lord Anguo and her day and night, and often sobbed for not being able to see them. His words flattered Lady Huayang, and gave her a positive impression of Zichu.

As for Lü Buwei, his part of the plan also revolved around setting the stage for Zichu's entrance into the political arena. He first purchased a large amount of expensive jewelry and other exotic items, and then requested to meet with Lady Huayang's elder sister. When he met with her, he presented her with the valuable items and begged her to entreat her younger sister on his behalf. "I have been told," the sister later said to Lady Huayang, "that the woman who has won a man's favor with her beauty will soon lose it when she is no longer young. Now your ladyship is serving Lord Anguo, and he loves you dearly, but you have no children of your own. You should select one of his

如果扶持国君，安定国家，那么，后世都可以享受其恩泽。我愿意去做。"

吕不韦决定资助子楚，帮助他继承秦国的王位。穷困潦倒的子楚听了吕不韦的计划，想都不敢想，不住地行礼，急切地说："如果真像您计划的那样，我愿分出秦国的土地与您共享。"

此时，秦昭襄（xiāng）王还在位，子楚的父亲还只是太子，被称为安国君。安国君有二十多个儿子，子楚既非长子，又不受宠爱，很难立为继承人。安国君宠爱华阳夫人，但华阳夫人没有生育孩子。这是一个绝好的机会。

从事商业经营、企业生产，现代汉语中称之为"经济"；从事安邦治国的活动，古代汉语中也称之为"经济"。经商与政治确实有许多共同点。吕不韦商业上的成功，很快转变为政治上的精明。

他一方面给子楚很多钱，让他广交社会贤达，获得良好的声誉。一方面又亲自来到秦都咸阳劝说华阳夫人。他极力赞扬子楚的贤德和智慧，并说子楚在赵国日夜思念安国君和华阳夫人，常常暗自流泪。华阳夫人非常高兴，开始对子楚有了好感。

吕不韦又花费许多金子购买大量的珍奇玩物，亲自带上，求见华阳夫人的姐姐，并通过她，说服华阳夫人。夫人的姐姐说："我听说，以美貌获得男人欢心的女人，一旦衰老，便失去了宠爱。今天夫人侍奉安国君，很受宠幸但却没有生育孩子，

many sons who is both worthy and capable, and has filial piety to you, and adopt him as your own child to make him the crown heir. If you do this, you will not only enjoy the same honor and respect from Lord Anguo while he is alive, but if he dies, you will still have great influence as the mother of the new king."

Her remark caught Lady Huayang's attention. She thought for some time and asked, "Who should I adopt?"

"Among the king's many sons, Zichu is worthy, capable and obedient. He knows that he is not the first born son and it is impossible for him to be the crown heir. What's more, his own mother fell into disfavor long ago. He is wholeheartedly willing to cling to your ladyship."

Lady Huayang accepted her sister's advice. At her earnest and repeated requests, Lord Anguo agreed to make Zichu the crown heir by granting him a token carved out of jade. Lord Anguo also assigned Lü Buwei to assist Zichu. From that time on, Zichu became well-known in all the states.

Lü Buwei had a young concubine named Zhao Ji, who was not only beautiful, but also skilled at singing and dancing. Shortly after she came to live with him, she became pregnant. One day Zichu was invited to Lü Buwei's house, and at dinner Lü asked Zhao Ji to dance for them. Enthralled by her exceeding beauty and graceful dancing steps, Zichu desperately fell in love with her. So when he was holding his cup to toast the host, he took the opportunity to request that Lü Buwei allow him to take Zhao Ji as his own concubine. At first Lü Buwei was angry, but once he calmed himself, he granted Zichu's request.

When Zichu and Zhao Ji began to live together, she said nothing about her pregnancy. Coincidentally, Zhao Ji's pregnancy lasted 12 months, and in the twelfth month she gave birth to a boy. The boy was born in 250 B.C., the 48th year of the reign of King Zhao Xiang of Qin. The month in which he was born happened to be the Chinese month zheng (正)—first of the year in the Chinese calendar then in use, and accordingly he received the given name Zheng (正). But in some ancient books this character was written as "政," hence his name "嬴政" (Ying Zheng).

This boy was none other than Emperor Qin Shihuang.

Now that Zichu had a son, he was so excited that he made Zhao Ji his legal wife.

Ying Zheng was born between the two great battles between the states Qin and Zhao. One year, in the first month, the two states made peace with each other and agreed upon a truce. But several months later, unwilling to fulfill the

不如趁早在安国君的公子中选一位贤能孝顺的人，当做自己亲生的儿子，立他为指定的继承人。安国君在世一日，夫人都会受到尊重，一旦安国君去世，夫人也会因为儿子是国君而不会丧失权势。"

华阳夫人听后恍然大悟，想了想问道："该收养哪一位呢？"

"几位公子当中，子楚既贤能，又有孝心。他自知论长幼当不上王位继承人，而他的母亲又失宠，愿意依附于夫人。"

华阳夫人听了，表示接受。随后，安国君答应了华阳夫人的请求，刻玉符为信物，确定子楚为王位的继承人，并请吕不韦辅助子楚。从此，子楚在各诸侯国的名声越来越大。

吕不韦有一个年轻的小妾（qiè）赵姬，姿容美丽，能歌善舞。同居不久，赵姬就怀有身孕。这一天，子楚在吕不韦家中做客，吕不韦让赵姬前来献舞伴酒。子楚见到赵姬天姿国色，舞姿动人，心生爱慕之情，于是举杯为吕不韦祝酒，并索要赵姬。吕不韦一听十分恼怒，但转念一想，还是压下怒气，答应了子楚的请求。

子楚高兴地把赵姬娶回了家，赵姬也不说已经怀有身孕。巧合的是，赵姬竟然怀孕了十二个月。她生下一个男孩，时间正好是秦昭襄王四十八年（公元前259年）的正（zhēng）月，因此，取名"正"，古书上经常写作"政"，故称"嬴政"。

他就是秦始皇。

子楚得了儿子，很高兴，立赵姬为夫人。

嬴政出生在秦国、赵国之间两次大战的间隙（jiàn xì）。这年正月，两国讲和停战。但数月之后，赵国拒不履行割让六

agreement that it should cede six towns to Qin, the Zhao State allied itself with the Qi State to launch an attack on Qin. In 257 B.C. (the 50th year of King Zhao Xiang of Qin), the Qin army besieged Handan again, placing the Zhao State in great danger. For this reason, the king of Zhao decided to kill Qin's hostage in Zhao—Zichu and his family.

When Lü Buwei heard the news, he tried to stop the Zhao King from doing so. "Zichu is the beloved son of the royal family of Qin," he said to the king, "and the Queen of Qin intends to make him the crown heir. If you killed him, Qin would have a perfect excuse to attack Zhao. In my humble opinion, you should send him back to Qin and help him to take the throne. Zichu will surely be grateful." But the Zhao king rejected Lü's proposal.

Failing to persuade the king of Zhao, Lü Buwei managed to bribe the jailors with 300 kilograms of gold, which enabled Zichu to escape from Zhao to the camp of the Qin army. Now Zichu could finally return to Xianyang, the capital of his home state. When the Zhao king was informed of Zichu's escape, he decided to kill Zhao Ji and her son out of revenge. But Zhao Ji came from a very rich and powerful family in Handan. Her family saved her by hiding Zhao Ji and her son away, and they both survived the perilous situation.

Lady Huayang's home state was the state of Chu. As such, after Zichu returned to Xianyang, he came to see her dressed in the traditional clothing of Chu. His deliberate behavior pleased Lady Huayang, and as a result Lord Anguo also began to think highly of Zichu.

Several years later, after King Zhao Xiang of Qin died, Lord Anguo came to the throne and Zichu became the official crown prince. After relation between Qin and Zhao improved, the Zhao State granted Zhao Ji the permission to go to the Qin State with her son. Before long, Lord Anguo died and Zichu succeeded to the throne, known as King Zhuang Xiang of Qin. Zhao Ji was made queen and Ying Zheng became the crown prince.

With Zichu's ascension to the throne, Lü Buwei's "rare-commodity" plan began to work. The king made Lü the prime minister—the highest official at the time—and also conferred on Lü Buwei the title Marquis of Wenxin with an estate that received 100 000 households' tribute in Luoyang, Henan Province.

But Zichu died only three years after he became king, and Ying Zheng ascended the throne in 247 B.C. at the age of 12. He also appointed Lü Buwei as his prime minister, and showed him great respect by calling him "Zhongfu," which means "my second father."

城的和约，还联合齐国一道对抗秦国。秦昭襄王五十年（公元前257年），秦国再派大军围攻邯郸。赵国形势危急，打算杀掉人质子楚。子楚一家面临灭顶之灾。

吕不韦得到消息后，设法阻拦赵王，他说："子楚是秦王室的宠子，当今王后欲立他为太子。如果赵国杀了子楚，秦国必定以此为借口进攻赵国。我看还不如将他放回秦国，使他登上王位，子楚必定感恩于赵国。"然而赵王并没有接受他的意见。

劝说无效，吕不韦用六百斤金子贿赂看守，使子楚得以逃脱，投奔秦国军队，最后回到秦都咸阳。赵王得知子楚逃走，便欲加害赵姬母子。赵姬是邯郸富豪之女，娘家人把赵姬母子藏了起来，最终躲过了这场劫难。

华阳夫人是楚国人，子楚回到咸阳后，便身穿楚国的服饰去拜见她。华阳夫人心里十分高兴，安国君对子楚也非常赏识。

几年之后，秦昭襄王去世，安国君即位，子楚为太子。这时秦、赵关系有所缓和，赵国便将赵姬母子送归秦国。可不久，安国君也去世了，子楚继承王位，后世称之为秦庄襄王。赵姬立为王后，嬴政为太子。

子楚即位，吕不韦最初所谓"奇货可居"的计划终于完成。吕不韦被任命为丞相，这是最高级别的官员；同时被封为文信侯，以河南洛阳十万户作为封地。

子楚在位时间不长，三年之后便去世了。公元前247年，十二岁的嬴政登上了秦国的王位。他尊崇吕不韦为相国，号称"仲父"，即相当于秦王的父亲。

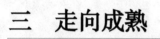

三　走向成熟

Chapter Ⅲ　Coming of Age

Though Ying Zheng was the king now, he was still a minor and could not yet deal with state affairs. Therefore, the Qin State was actually ruled by Zhao Ji, the queen mother, and Lü Buwei, the prime minister.

When the Qin King was young, Lü Buwei and Zhao Ji were rather unscrupulous about their adultery. But as the king matured, Lu Buwei began to worry about his immoral relationship with Zhao Ji for fear that their adultery might someday have disastrous results. To protect himself, Lü Buwei took in a lascivious man named Lao Ai and asked Lao Ai to replace him as the queen mother's lover. In order to deceive the public, Lü Buwei had someone bring a false charge against Lao Ai, for which Lao Ai was sentenced to castration, a cruel form of punishment that can permanently damage a man's procreative ability. But the queen mother bribed the executioner, and Lao Ai was spared this cruelty. Instead, he merely had his beard pulled out. Ever since then Lao Ai became the queen mother's harem attendant—a eunuch, as it was assumed that the castration succeeded. Owing to her continued illicit relationship with Lao Ai, Queen Mother Zhao successively gave birth to two sons.

As the sweetheart of Queen Mother Zhao, Lao Ai was conferred the title "Marquis of Changxin" and was favored of the queen mother. He became so rich and powerful that he even maintained an army of minions and servants that numbered in the thousands. He even plotted with the queen mother that once the present Qin King died, their own son would be the successor.

One day, when gambling and drinking with the other princes and ministers, Lao Ai was involved in a drunken quarrel. With his eyes open wide he shouted, "I am the stepfather of our king. How dare you—a poor sirrah— defy me?" On hearing this, the man who quarreled with Lao Ai immediately reported this to the Qin King. "Lao Ai is no eunuch," the man said. "He has continued his relationship with the queen mother, and she has given birth to two sons in secret, whom they plan to place on the throne." Ying Zheng at once ordered his men to look into the matter. The investigation proved that this was true, but Ying Zheng did not take any immediate action.

In 238 B.C., about the ninth years after Ying Zheng came to the throne, he turned 21 years old. According to tradition, Ying Zheng should hold his coronation in the ancestral temple, a sign of his maturity as king. The ancestral temple of Qin was in the city of Yong, the former capital city of the state, where several generations of the kings of Qin had ruled for nearly 300 years. Now in order to hold the ceremony the present Qin King came all the way from Xianyang to the city of Yong. In the ceremony the king put on the crown and carried a long sword, which meant that he would reign over his kingdom in person.

秦王嬴政少年即位，还没有处理国政的能力。因此，秦国朝政就由太后赵姬和相国吕不韦执掌。

秦王年少，吕不韦不时与太后赵姬私通，并没有太多顾忌。可随着嬴政年龄的增长，吕不韦担心起来，唯恐事情败露，灾祸及身，于是把一向纵情声色的嫪毐（lào ǎi）收为自己的门客。不久，就将嫪毐送给太后。为掩人耳目，吕不韦派人诬告嫪毐犯罪，将处以宫刑。这是使男子不能生育的一种酷刑。由于太后贿赂（huì lù）行刑者，嫪毐并未受到酷刑，仅被拔掉脸上的胡须，成了太后的贴身侍从——宦（huàn）官。赵太后与嫪毐私通，先后生下了两个孩子。

嫪毐富贵发达，被封为长信侯，得到了很多赏赐，权势很大，家中门客奴仆竟有几千人之多。嫪毐与太后密谋，一旦秦王去世，就由他们的儿子继承王位。

一日，嫪毐与王公大臣们饮酒赌博，醉酒之后，与人争执起来。只见他圆睁双目，大声喝斥："我是当今国王的继父，你这穷小子怎敢与我对抗！"争执者赶紧逃走，报告秦王说："嫪毐实际上不是宦官，他与太后私通，已生下两个儿子，都隐藏着，密谋让自己的儿子继承王位。"嬴政一听，立即派官员调查，果然如此，但他并没有立刻采取行动。

秦王九年（公元前238年），嬴政二十一岁。按照礼仪，他必须在祖宗的宗庙里接受冠礼。这是长大成人的标志。秦国的宗庙在雍（yōng）城，那是秦国过去的都城，历代秦王在这里经营了近三百年，宗庙都在这里。秦王从咸阳来到雍城，举行冠礼仪式。他头戴王冠，身佩长剑。这意味着他即将亲理朝政。

Meanwhile, Lao Ai discovered that the king was secretly investigating him. In fearful desperation, Lao Ai became reckless. Since the king was in the city of Yong, he took the opportunity to incite a rebellion against the king. Lao Ai first forged the seals of the king and queen mother, and with these seals he gathered soldiers from among the local troops, including court bodyguards and cavalrymen as well as his own toadies. He then attacked the Qin Palace in Yong, the temporary residence of the king.

When informed of Lao Ai's attempt, King Ying Zheng took decisive action and assembled his troops, and soon quenched the rebellion. Lao Ai and his followers were captured, and the king ordered his men to put Lao Ai to death by turning him asunder by five horse-drawn carts. Lao Ai's entire family was exterminated, including his two sons born by the queen mother, who were also the half brothers of the king. In addition, by the king's order, 20 of Lao Ai's most trusted followers were decapitated and about 4 000 households of Lao Ai's cronies were exiled to the place of Shu.*

Even though Ying Zheng was only 21 years old, his actions convincingly demonstrated his statesmanship and unique style of governance.

Perhaps because he thought his mother had disgraced him, the king ordered that she be banished to the city of Yong. All his ministers and servants tried to persuade him to reconsider, as it went against the traditional standards of filial piety for a son to banish his own mother. The king was so vexed by their persuasion that he swore that anyone who tried to intercede with him for the queen mother would be summarily executed. According to the historical records, there were 27 court officials who pleaded for the queen mother, and the king had them all killed.

In spite of this, a man called Mao Jiao from the State of Qi insisted on discussing this matter with the king. The king sent someone to ask him whether or not he had seen the 27 dead bodies before the palace.

Mao Jiao's reply was: "It is said that there are 28 constellations in the heaven. Now 27 people were killed, and I am willing to be the 28th so that we can make a complete collection of constellations. As you can see, I do not fear death."

The king was furious. "This man is violating my injunction on purpose," he said. "Prepare me a giant stockpot! I'll boil him alive."

Mao Jiao walked slowly toward the king and when he came near, he stopped and saluted the king with a kowtow. "I hear," said he, "that just as men in life do not take the discussion of death as taboo, rulers of states should not take the discussion of the collapse of states as taboo. Men who fear death

　　很快有人把秦王派人调查的事情告诉了嫪毐。嫪毐十分惶恐，决定铤（tǐng）而走险，利用秦王在雍城的机会发动叛乱。他伪造秦王御玺（yùxǐ）和太后玺，即君主与太后的印章，召集部分地方士兵、宫中侍卫、骑兵和自己的门客，企图攻打嬴政在雍城的行宫——蕲（qí）年宫。

　　秦王嬴政听到消息，调集兵马，采取果断的措施，平息了叛乱。嫪毐及其同伙很快便全部落网。秦王下令：车裂嫪毐，他的宗族全被灭绝。太后与嫪毐所生的两个儿子——嬴政的同母弟弟，也被处死。嫪毐的亲信党羽共二十人被斩首，其门客四千余家流放到蜀地。

　　秦王嬴政这年刚刚二十一岁，充分显露出非凡的政治才能和独特的统治风格。

　　也许，秦王再也不想见到令他羞愧无比的母亲，于是下令将她迁到雍城居住。大臣们纷纷阻止此事，因为儿子囚母，违背中国传统的孝道。嬴政十分恼怒，下令：谁敢再为太后说情，一律处死。史书上记载，先后为太后求情的二十七个人，全被秦王杀了。

　　但有个叫茅焦的齐国人，仍然执意要进谏秦王。嬴政传话说："他没有看见二十七具尸体堆放在宫门前吗？"

　　茅焦说："天上有二十八星宿（xiù），现在被杀者二十七人，我是来凑这二十八星宿之数的。我岂是怕死之人？"

　　秦王大怒道："这是故意违反我的禁令。准备汤锅，我要活烹（pēng）了他！"

　　茅焦慢慢地走上前去，再次叩头，说："我听说，活着的人不避讳死亡，治国的人不避讳国家的灭亡；害怕死亡的人不

---

* Sichuan province in China used to be called Shu, which is the most inaccessible area in China even today.

cannot enjoy a long life, and rulers who fear that their state will collapse cannot ensure its prolonged existence. Live or die, survive or perish, these are things that all sages must consider. Will Your Majesty allow me to say something about them?"

The king softened himself a little and said, "Go ahead and say it."

"The Qin State is endeavoring to unify the whole of China," Mao Jiao continued, "but as its king, Your Majesty has confined his own mother in the city of Yong. If all the lords and righteous persons have heard of what you have done to your mother, I fear they will withdraw their support of your rule."

King Ying Zheng accepted Mao Jiao's advice and he went to the city of Yong in person to bring the queen mother back to Xianyang, the Qin capital. He also appointed Mao Jiao to an important post of the state.

Mao Jiao was a man of courage and resourcefulness. He persuaded the king to change the mind by using his own ambition to unify China, which not only preserved his life, but also helped him to win the king's trust and attain an important position in the royal government. Despite recently coming to power, instead of being arrogant, obstinate, or opinionated, King Ying Zheng willingly accepted others' advice. He severely punished rebels and showered honor and praise on those who provided him with good advice, demonstrating the young king's capacity for handling government affairs.

Lü Buwei, of course, had much to do with Lao Ai's rebellion, and Ying Zheng had to decide how to deal with his deception and treachery. However, at that time, Lü still held the position of prime minister and had an estate of 100 000 households in Luoyang. He was not only powerful in the Qin State, but was also very influential in the other states. He made friends with many able and virtuous people and had as many as three thousand courtiers, and these people had formed a political force of no small influence. Seeing as the state had just crushed a rebellion, King Ying Zheng held that it would be improper to kill a prestigious minister immediately, as if he killed Lü Buwei, greater disturbances might arise. For this reason, the king chose not to punish Lü Buwei.

About one year later, when the situation in the state stabilized, King Ying Zheng dismissed Lü Buwei from his post and sent him home to his estate in Luoyang. While in Luoyang, Lü Buwei still received many guests and messengers who brought him good will from lords of other states. The king began to worry that Lü Buwei might collude with his enemies, both in Qin and in other states, and might start another rebellion. So he wrote an upbraiding letter to Lü Buwei, in which he said:

能长生，害怕灭亡的国家不能长存。生死存亡是圣贤关注的事情，陛下是否愿意听呢？"

秦王改变了态度，说道："你说吧。"

茅焦说："秦国正致力于统一天下，大王却将母亲囚禁在雍城，天下诸侯义士如果听说这事，恐怕便不会再向着秦国了。"

嬴政于是亲自把母亲迎回咸阳，并让茅焦担任重要的官职。

茅焦富有胆略，他以秦国统一天下的目标说服了秦王，不但没有惹来杀身之祸，反而获得了重用。此时的嬴政虽刚刚亲政，但从善如流。他严厉惩罚乱党，褒奖进谏人士，一惩一奖，显示出年轻的嬴政已经具备处理政事的能力。

嫪毐之祸很自然地牵连到吕不韦。但他身为相国，有洛阳十万户的封邑，位高权重，在诸侯国中享有很高的声誉。他广纳贤才，有门客三千人，确实形成了一股不小的政治势力。秦王考虑到一场叛乱刚刚平息，如果随之诛杀声望很高的大臣，恐怕会引起更大的震荡，于是暂时不提治罪的事情。

大约过了一年，形势稍稍平稳，秦王才免去了吕不韦相国一职，让他回到洛阳的封地居住。吕不韦回到洛阳封地，仍有诸侯国派遣宾客和使者前往问候。秦始皇担心他内外勾结，图谋叛乱，于是亲自给他写了一封信，责问他：

"What contribution have you made to our state? Nothing. But from our state you have gained an estate of 100 000 households' tribute in Henan. Do you have any kinship with our royal family? No. Yet you are called 'Zhongfu.' I hereby command you to leave Luoyang and take your family to Shu."

By the king's order, Lü Buwei departed for Shu. Lü knew very well that the king would never pardon him for what he had done, and that Ying Zheng would kill him sooner or later. Fearing the king's vengeance, Lü Buwei committed suicide by drinking poisoned wine. The poison in the wine is called "Zhen," which according to legend is made from the feathers of a kind of poisonous birds.

Lü Buwei underwent many dramatic changes in his life: At one time he was one of the most rich and powerful men in the Chinese world, but his life ended in tragedy. He had a shrewd mind and was skilled at scheming, helping Zichu ascend the throne and making himself eminent and powerful. But even with power, wealth and fame, he still failed to continue as he had started. Lü Buwei could be said to have lacked sincerity; whereas sincerity cannot always ensure fortune or happiness, insincerity is a sure recipe for disaster.

When Lu Buwei died, the young king was only 23 years old. Young as he was, he eliminated two powerful political groups headed by Lao Ai and Lü Buwei within two years, and held the power of the state firmly in his own hands. What he had done laid a solid political foundation for his annexation of the six other states years later.

Shortly after the king quenched Lao Ai's rebellion, the Qin State issued an order for all the guests (i.e., the people who were not the natives of Qin) to leave the state. The order probably originated in the espionage of the state of Zheng.

Since Ying Zheng came to the throne, he had started several wars. Han, Zhao and Wei were the three states which lay closely to the east of Qin. They had all lost land to Qin, and the kings of these three states lived in a state of constant fear. The Han State was surrounded by those powerful states of Qin, Chu, Zhao and Wei, and it remained constantly on watch for wars or conflicts with those states. The king of Han knew that the Qin King was ambitious and loved large-scale construction. So he conceived a plot which he called "the plot to exhaust the strength of Qin." According to this plot, they would encourage Qin to start large-scale civil engineering projects, thus draining their manpower and resources so that Qin could not afford another war.

The Han State then began to put this somewhat naive plan into action. They sent a hydraulic engineer named Zheng Guo to Qin as a spy. His mission

"你有什么功劳，秦国却封赏你河南十万户？你与秦国有什么亲缘关系，竟被称为'仲父'？你不要住在洛阳了，带着你的家人到蜀地去吧！"

秦王下令将吕不韦全家迁往蜀地。吕不韦意识到秦王决不会放过他，终究难逃一死，于是便饮鸩（zhèn）自尽了。"鸩"，传说是用一种毒鸟的羽毛制成的毒酒。

吕不韦的一生充满戏剧性：曾经显贵无比，最终却以悲剧结束。头脑精明，善于经营，把子楚一步步地扶上王位，自己也获得了显赫的权势，拥有权力、财富和声誉，但却不能为自己的下半生周密安排。正如前人所批评的那样，他缺乏真诚。真诚虽然不能永远带来幸运，但虚假最终会遭遇不幸。

年仅二十三岁的秦始皇在短短的两年时间里，就先后清除了嫪毐、吕不韦两大势力集团，把大权紧紧掌握在自己手中。这为秦国吞灭六国打下了坚实的政治基础。

嫪毐事件刚刚结束时，秦国就发生了"逐客"事件。此事最早可能与郑国间谍案有关。

嬴政登上王位后，不断发动战争。韩、赵、魏三国紧紧靠着秦国的东面，在与秦国多次交战中，不断地丧失成片的国土，三国的君主惊恐不安。韩国夹在秦、楚、赵、魏等强国的中间，疲于应付，备受兵战之苦。韩王知道秦王好（hào）大喜功，热衷于大兴土木，于是想了一个"疲秦"之计。这个计谋，就是促使秦国兴建浩大的土木工程，这样，耗尽其人力物力，那么它就没有力量再发动战争了。

韩国真的实施了这一项听起来有些天真的计划。他们派遣

was to persuade Qin into constructing irrigation systems by digging a long canal. The canal, more than 300 *li* *(75 miles or 120 kilometers) long, would branch off the Jing River and feed into the Luo River in the east, and once completed, it could irrigate much farmland. Since the rainfall in Guanzhong region of Qin was very limited, people in this area frequently suffered from drought. That was why the government of the Qin State placed so much importance on irrigation. Soon the officials of the Qin State adopted Zheng Guo's suggestion about digging the canal. It did require many people and resources to work on the project, but by the time they were half finished, Zheng Guo was found to be a spy. The king ordered his men to have Zheng Guo put to death, and the project was halted.

Facing the death penalty, Zheng Guo said calmly and frankly, "At first, I did come here as a spy, but if the canal can be completed, it will truly benefit your people. Yes, what I did might keep the Han State alive for years, but could benefit Qin for ages."

The king found Zheng Guo's defense reasonable, and therefore permitted him to continue the project. The project was finally completed. Thanks to this ambitious project the canal could irrigate 40 000 hectares of farmland in the Guanzhong region of Shanxi. As a result, the production of the farmlands in and around this area surged. According to historical records, "the soil in the Guanzhong region was fertile, and no famine occurred for years." As a result of this project, the Qin State thrived like it never had before, providing ample material support for the forthcoming unification of China. The canal was named "Zhengguoqu" (the Zhengguo Canal) , also called "Zhengqu" (Zheng Canal).

The intrigue surrounding Zheng Guo, however, aroused Qin's suspicion of people from other states. Zheng Guo, Lao Ai and Lü Buwei were all not Qin natives, and their actions had severely threatened state security. Some members of the royal family, as well as some high-ranking Qin officials, had always held grudges against foreigners who held important positions in the Qin State, and they took this opportunity to advise the king against them. They told him, "Those people professed that they came to swear allegiance to the Qin King, but they actually came for their own king's benefit, plotting and scheming to drive wedges between the ministers and officials of the Qin State. We beg Your Majesty to stop further treachery, and drive these people from our state."

Under this pressure, the king gave the order to expel all the foreign guests from the Qin State. By this order, a large-scale search was done all over the state, and all the people from the other states were expelled.

一位名叫郑国的水利工程师作为间谍，劝说秦国兴修水利，开掘一条很长的河渠。这条河渠分流泾水，东注洛水，全长三百多里（75英里或120千米），用以灌溉农田。秦国的关中地区降水量少，经常发生旱灾，所以秦国一向重视水利建设。他们一听这项兴建河渠的计划，很快就采纳了。修建这条水渠，确实消耗了秦国大量的劳力和财力。工程进行到一半的时候，郑国的间谍身份暴露了。秦国打算处死郑国，并终止这项水利工程。

郑国面临死刑，非常坦诚地说："我起初确实是作为间谍来到秦国，但如果此渠能够建成，必会给秦国带来巨大的利益。我为韩国延长了几年的寿命，却为秦国建立了万世之功。"

秦国听从了郑国的辩解，命令他继续主持这项水利工程。河渠完成，使陕西关中四万余顷农田得到灌溉，农业生产力得到提高，史书记载"关中为沃野，无凶年"。秦国因此更为富强，为统一天下奠定了物质基础。这条河渠被命名为"郑国渠"，也称"郑渠"。

但这件事却使得秦国人对从其他诸侯国来的士人产生了很大的怀疑。郑国、嫪毐、吕不韦等都不是秦国人，他们的行为确实威胁到了秦国的安全。秦国的宗室大臣一直不满他国人在秦国担任要职，借此机会向秦王进谏说，各诸侯国的人来到秦国，声称为秦王效忠，其实大多是为自己的君主进行游说（shuì）离间（jiàn）等阴谋活动，请大王把所有的这些人驱逐出境。

在众大臣的建议下，嬴政颁布了"逐客令"。在秦国范围内，大规模搜索，驱逐所有的外来客。

---

* *li*: the Chinese unit of length, one *li* is about 0.5 kilometer.

Among those people was a man named Li Si, who came from the Chu State and formerly served Lü Buwei. By the time the order to expel all the foreign guests was issued, he was a senior official of Qin and was valued by the king. On his way to leave Qin, he sent a letter to the king explaining that expelling all the foreigners would do harm to the state. The letter is one of his best-known pieces, entitled "Jian Zhu Ke Shu" ("Memorial Opposing the Expulsion of Foreigners").

In his letter, Li Si first cited some examples of several deceased kings since the time of King Mu of Qin. All these kings were courageous enough to assign foreigners to important posts, such as Shang Yang, Zhang Yi and Fan Sui, etc., and because of the daring acts of these late kings, Qin gradually became more and more powerful. Then Li Si pointed out that the present Qin King appreciated the jewelry, women, songs, dances and music of other states but belittled their people's competence. This ran contrary to what a wise king should do if he desired to conquer other states. Li Si concluded his letter by warning the king that this order would have dire consequences: Persons of outstanding abilities would all go to serve the enemy states, which would weaken the national power of the Qin State. Inside the state, the king would lose the support of his subjects, and outside the state, he would find many new enemies. It would be impossible for such a state to remain dominant and safe from its foes.

When he finished reading Li Si's letter, the Qin King felt as if he was awakened from a dream. He had the "order for guests to leave" withdrawn at once and also sent someone to call back Li Si. When Li Si returned, the king reinstated him to his post. Ever since then, Li Si became one of Ying Zheng's most trusted advisers. Over the course of unifying the country and constructing the Qin Empire, Li Si was central to many state policies, including military conquest.

During the Warring States Period, the states not only contended for land and populace, but for talented individuals. The Qin State was formerly a small state in northwest China, but because it could properly employ men of worth, it rose rapidly and became a state which could defy any of the powerful states among China's central plains. Despite the young king's headstrong personality, he knew enough to accept good advice, and when he was wrong he corrected his mistakes without hesitation. From Li Si's petition, he realized the importance of talented individuals to his own state, and ever after he always elevated people of talent to high positions, regardless of their place of birth. For this reason, many outstanding people in other states came to Qin to help

有一位很受秦王重视的官员李斯，也在被驱逐之列。他是楚国人，起初为吕不韦的门客，此时已经成了秦国的高级官员。他在离开秦国的路上，给秦王嬴政写了一封信，恳切地指出逐客令将对秦国产生不利的影响。这就是著名的《谏逐客书》。

文中首先列举了秦穆（mù）公以来的几位先王，大胆任用商鞅（yāng）、张仪、范睢（suī）等一批外来客，使秦国国力逐步强大起来的事实。接着又指出，秦王喜欢他国所产的珍宝、美女、歌舞和音乐，却轻视其他国家的人才，这种重物轻人的做法，完全违背了英明的君主成就帝业、一统天下的政策。最后，李斯指出逐客令必将造成的严重后果：将天下的英才送给敌国，削弱秦国自身的力量，内失民心，外结仇怨，这样的国家想要避免危险，完全办不到。

秦王读完此信，如梦方醒，立即宣布废除逐客令，并派人追回李斯，恢复他的官职。从此，李斯成了嬴政的主要谋臣。在统一天下以及建立秦帝国的过程中，他出谋划策，制定各项政治措施，起到了重要的作用。

战国之际，各诸侯国斗争激烈，不仅争夺土地和人口，而且也争夺人才。秦国原来是地处西北的一个小国，后来一跃成为与中原大国相抗衡的国家，得益于它对人才的重用。这位年轻的国君虽然专断，但能听从好的意见，知错就改。从李斯的劝谏中，他认识到人才对秦国的重要性，此后颇能重用人才。其他诸侯国的优秀人才纷纷来到秦国，协助嬴政谋划天下，在

King Ying Zheng carry out his goal to conquer the other states.

In his collection of poems "*Archaistic Poetry*," Li Bai, the great poet of the Tang Dynasty, glorified the courage and insight displayed by Qin Shihuang in his war to unify China with one of his poems. The poem praises the might of the Qin King in annexing the six states and unifying the country. Li Bai wrote that with a swipe of his sward, the Qin King quelled resistance and forced them to submit; his actions only serve to manifest his distinctive wisdom and capacity.

It took Qin Shihuang only 10 years to wipe out the six states of Han, Zhao, Wei, Chu, Yan and Qi in the east, which had existed for several hundred years. The Qin army swept away all these obstacles to unification and captured the kings of these six states. The nobilities and servants of these states all became subjects of the Qin Empire. Within a very short time, peace and order were reestablished.

But why could Qin Shihuang unify China in such a short time? The first reason is that the Qin army consisted of brave and skilled warriors. Another equally important reason was that Qin Shihuang was a master of strategy, and carried it out with utmost efficiency. His strategy was to bribe the ministers of those states with gold and valuables to estrange his enemy states. In addition, the Qin State also allied with the states further away from them to attack the states nearest them so that the distant states would not support the states adjacent to Qin. Thanks to this policy, the Qin State annexed its three neighboring states—Han, Zhao, and Wei—one by one. When the three states were annexed, Qin began to attack the states at its both sides—the states of Yan and Chu. After that, its army pressed eastward and wiped out the last state—the Qi State, and when Qi fell, unification was achieved.

This strategic policy did not originate from the King, but from a strategist named Wei Liao. Wei Liao came from the city of Da Liang of the Wei State (the present day city of Kaifeng in Henan Province) and was an expert on the art of war, having penned the famous *Master Wei Liao Zi* (or *Art of War*). In this book he depicted in great detail various forms of battle array. Some scholars hold that the forms he depicted are much like those of the terracotta warriors and horses which were unearthed in modern times. Wei Liao offered his advice and suggestions to the Qin King shortly after he came to Xianyang. At that time, the king had just withdrawn his order to expel foreigners, and feared that because of this order he had offended foreigners of talent, so he accepted an audience with Wei Liao. When the king asked him about the general situation, Wei Liao said,

帝国的崛起中建功立业。

唐代诗人李白的诗歌《古风》第三首，赞扬秦始皇在统一战争中表现出来的气魄：

秦王扫六合，虎视何雄哉！

挥剑决浮云，诸侯尽西来。

明断自天启，大略驾群才。

意思是说，秦王嬴政吞并六国、虎视天下是何等的威武！长剑一挥，诸侯国纷纷俯首称臣。这些都是因为秦始皇具有超凡的智慧和才能。

秦始皇仅用了十年时间，就吞并了经营几百年的东方六国。秦军所向披靡（mǐ），韩、赵、魏、楚、燕、齐的国君相继成了秦始皇的俘虏，各国的贵族大臣也都成了秦帝国的臣民。弹（tán）指之间，天下大定。

秦始皇之所以能够如此神速地统一天下，除了秦军的勇猛善战之外，还与他采取有效的策略有重要的关系。秦国的策略是，用金银财宝贿赂各国大臣，破坏各国之间的联盟。一方面进攻邻近的国家，另一方面与远方的诸侯国保持良好的关系，使他们不再支持那些邻近的国家。这个"远交近攻"的战略，使秦国首先吞并相邻的韩、赵、魏三国，再攻其两翼——燕国和楚国，最后挺军东进，灭掉最东边的齐国，完成统一大业。

这个战略策划，并非秦王自己设想出来的，而是来自于一位军事家尉缭（wèi liáo）的构想。尉缭是魏国大梁（今河南开封）人，对兵法很有研究，著有《尉缭子》。书中描述的兵阵形式，有学者认为，与现代出土的秦始皇兵马俑的布局基本一致。尉缭一到咸阳，就为秦王嬴政献计献策。由于嬴政刚刚撤销了逐客令，唯恐怠（dài）慢了天下英才，连忙请尉缭入朝。秦王问他对当前天下大势有何看法，尉缭说：

"At present, the Qin State is so large and powerful that the other states are merely counties in comparison. Yet I fear that if these states unite, then they could gather an army great enough to threaten even Qin. Therefore, I advise that Your Majesty use gold and jewelry to bribe the powerful officials in these states. In this way, you can sow dissension among these states and preempt their alliance. You might have to spend no more than 300 000 *liang** gold on bribery, but this will enable you to wipe out these states one by one."

Ying Zheng heartily applauded Wei Liao's strategy and was deeply impressed by Wei's military talent. He took action immediately by sending spies to estrange one state from another and at the same time he spared no effort in driving wedges between the kings from their ministers and servants.

The first time Wei Liao saw the Qin King, he was surprised by what he saw. According to tradition, as a king, he could enjoy the best food, clothes, chariots, guards of honor, and so on, but King Ying Zheng showed none of these before Wei Liao. Instead, he received Wei Liao as his equal by wearing the same clothes and eating the same food as Wei did. This made Wei Liao uneasy. He said, "The Qin King, with big eyes, a long nose, a prominent chest like an eagle's, and leopard voice, is an ambitious and ruthless person lacking in righteousness and mercy. Such a man, when in frustration, might be very humble, but once he has achieved his ambition, he could become dangerous. I am only a nobody, yet he behaved humbly before me. I suspect that when he has conquered all the six states, he will enslave the populace. I dare not stay near such a king for long." So Wei Liao left Qin without saying goodbye to anyone. When the king discovered Wei Liao was leaving, he at once sent his men to chase Wei down. His men brought Wei Liao back, and the king appointed him the commander-in-charge, the highest officer of the Qin military. In the wars for unification, Wei Liao was extremely instrumental in the counsels that he gave the king.

In the 13th year of his reign (234 B.C.), Ying Zheng ordered his army to launch an attack on the Han State. The purpose of the war was not for land or gold and valuables, but for a man named Han Fei, and the king demanded that Han give up Han Fei to him. But why should Qin start a war for Han Fei, a man of little importance at that time? It was due to a book that Han Fei wrote.

Han Fei was a member of the ruling family of Han. Both he and Li Si were pupils of Xunzi, the famous Confucian philosopher of that time. Han Fei was a man of great learning and ability, and also an excellent reader of classical works. He had thoroughly studied the theories of Daoism and Legalism, and had formed a political strategy of his own. A speech impediment

"当今的秦国已经很强大了，其他诸侯国不过是秦国所属的郡县罢了，但是我担心诸侯国联合起来，聚集力量，对秦发动突然袭击。我建议大王不要吝（lìn）惜财物，要用大量的财宝收买六国的权臣，破坏诸侯之间的联盟，扰乱各国的战略部署。贿赂的花费不会超过三十万金，但各诸侯国就可以逐一消灭了。"

嬴政十分赞同他的战略构想，赏识他的军事才能。于是派出间谍，离间诸侯之间和诸侯国内部君臣的关系。

尉缭初次见到秦王时，十分惊讶。因为按照传统，君王在饮食、服饰、车驾、仪仗等方面都享有最高的等级，可是，秦王却没有以君臣之礼接见尉缭，衣服饮食与尉缭的一样。这使尉缭很不安。尉缭说："秦王这个人，高鼻子，大眼睛，胸脯像鹰一样突出，声音像豺狼一样嘶哑。这种人不行恩惠，心性像虎狼一样凶狠。不得志的时候很谦恭，得志的时候一定非常狠毒。我只是一个普通人，但他却非常谦卑。如果秦王将来取得天下，天下人都会成为他的奴隶。不能与这样的君王相处太久。"尉缭不辞而别，离开了秦国。秦王发觉后，急忙派人追回尉缭，执意说服他留下，并任命他为秦国的最高军事统帅，负责全国的军事事务。在后来统一六国的战争中，尉缭出谋划策，起到了很大的作用。

秦王十三年（公元前234年），嬴政下令进攻韩国。这次秦军攻势强大，但却不是为了侵占土地、掠夺财宝，而是要求韩国交出韩非这个人。秦国为什么要大动干戈，讨要一个在韩国没有什么影响的人物呢？因为，韩非所著的书打动了秦王。

韩非是韩国的王室贵族，他和李斯都是当时著名的学者荀况的学生。韩非博学多才，熟读经典，对道家、法家的学说有

---

* *liang*: a unit of weight, approximately equal to 50 gram.

was reputed to have incited him to focus on writing. His deep insight and unusual literary talent made him outshine even Li Si.

Unlike Li Si, who went to Qin after he had completed his education, Han Fei returned to his native state. But the Han State was then in its declining years. The state was not ruled by the king, and instead was governed by ministers and officials. During the turmoil of facing a rising Qin State, the political situation was chaotic and unstable. Han Fei was so concerned over the future of his state that he wrote to the king many times. In his letters he strongly advocated that the king should rule the state by laws and employ people according to their worth. But the king of Han did not heed his advice. Han Fei was snubbed and even mocked for his concern over the state. Feeling bitter at heart, he wrote down his thoughts in several essays, such as "Loneliness and Anger" and "Five Kinds of Harmful People." In these essays he expressed his view on the political situation at that time and discussed how a king should rule his state.

Soon the Qin King read some of Han Fei's writings, and even though he did not know who had penned them, he was deeply impressed. When he finished "Loneliness and Anger" and "Five Kinds of Harmful People," he was struck with admiration and said to his men, "If I could get to know this man, I would die with nothing to regret."

"These essays were written by Han Fei," Li Si told the king.

"Where is Han Fei?"

"In the Han State."

So in order to get Han Fei, Qin Shihuang asked his army to make an attack on Han.

The king of Han never thought highly of Han Fei. Once the attacking Qin army had reached the place near his palace, the king at once dispatched Han Fei as an envoy to negotiate with Qin. Thus the Qin King withdrew his army, taking Han Fei with them.

Han Fei held that state governance should be based on an autocratic and centralized power. In the central government, the king should possess the supreme power and he should have an absolute control over the local authorities. Only in this way could a stable social order be maintained. In his opinion, when a king possessed supreme power, he could exercise control over his state, and when the king administered proper rewards and just punishment, he would become powerful. First, the king should create an ideal law system. Thus, in accordance with the law, those who obeyed the law should be rewarded, and those who violated it should be punished. Law formed the base

认真的研究，具有一整套的治国理论。他口吃而不善言辞，但擅长（shàn cháng）著述，其见识和文采连李斯也自叹不如。

学业完成之后，他没有像李斯那样来到秦国实现自己的抱负，而是回到自己的故国。但此时韩国日渐衰败，权臣当道，政坛混乱，在强秦的威胁之下，面临着亡国的危险。韩非内心十分焦虑，多次上书韩王，主张以法治国，任人唯贤。然而，韩王并不重用他，对他的意见也置之不理。韩非忧患之心遭到冷落和嘲讽，内心十分苦闷，写下了《孤愤》、《五蠹（dù）》等文章，共十多万字，发表自己对当时政治形势的见解，讨论君主统治的方法。

韩非的这些文章后来传到秦国。秦王并不知道这是什么人写的文章，但他读到《孤愤》、《五蠹》，却被深深地吸引，感叹说："唉呀！我如果能与这个人交往，那么，死也没有什么遗憾的了！"

李斯说："这是韩非写的书。"

"韩非现在何处？"

"在韩国。"

于是，秦始皇下令攻打韩国，要找到韩非。

韩王从没有重用过韩非，也不觉得他是多么了不起的人才。秦军兵临城下，韩王立即让韩非作为使臣前往秦国。秦军这才退去。

韩非主张，国家的治理必须依靠专制的中央集权。在中央，君王必须拥有至高无上的权力；在地方，中央拥有绝对的领导权，这样才能够维持稳定的社会秩序。他说，君主之所以能够掌控天下，是因为拥有令人生畏的权势。赏与罚使君主获得权势，对什么样的情况给予赏和罚必须由法律预先规定。因此，法是维护国家秩序的根本制度，任何人都必须遵守。他告诫君

of social order in a state, and to maintain the order, all should be required to abide by the law. He advised that a king should purge his mind of desires and ambitions and should not become too intimate with his ministers and officials or mingle himself with them. The king must remain aloof so that he can be impartial in his administration of justice. All of Han Fei's theories held to one precondition, that is, the king was always a wise and benevolent man.

　　Qin Shihuang, who totally identified with Han Fei's view, was eager to unify China and was also seeking absolute power and dominance. Han Fei's philosophy laid a theoretical foundation for the various administrative measures that the government took after the Qin State unified China.

主要清静寡（guǎ）欲，深居简出；没有嗜（shì）欲，臣下就无法投其所好，君主就能处于主动的地位。当然，韩非的理论前提是君主总是圣明的。

韩非的主张对于渴望一统天下、追求绝对权力的秦始皇而言，无疑十分合拍。他的观点，为秦国统一中国后所采取的各项行政措施，提供了重要的理论基础。

韩非画像

Portrait of Han Fei

四 吞并六国

Chapter Ⅳ　Annexation of the Six States

After he came to the Qin State, Han Fei wrote to the king on behalf of his native land, claiming that the Han State had been submissive to Qin for more than 30 years, and was nothing more than a county of Qin's. At present, Qin's greatest enemy was the Zhao State. Small as Han was, it was still unlikely that Qin could wipe it out completely if the Han people united against them to defend their towns and cities. And if the Qin army withdrew from Han without a complete victory, the other states would follow Han's example, and would resist Qin's incursions. If Han decided to renounce Qin and ally itself with the states of Zhao, Wei and Qi, things would become difficult for the king.

While Ying Zheng appreciated Han Fei's talent and capacity, he had doubts about his loyalty, and thus Han Fei's counsel fell on deaf ears.

Li Si and Han Fei formerly studied under the same teacher. "Han Fei is a prince of Han," said Li Si to the Qin King. "Now that Qin wishes to annex Han, it is only natural for Han Fei to defend his home state, so the Qin State clearly cannot employ such a man. But if we send him back, he will become a threat to Qin. We must find an excuse to have him killed."

Another man named Yao Jia was eventually responsible for Han Fei's death. Yao Jia used to be a gatekeeper in the Wei State, a lowlife street thief who moved to Zhao, but was driven out of there as well. However, this notorious criminal won the favor of the Qin King after he came to Qin, and was offered a high government post. Han Fei once mentioned to the Qin King that such a man could not be trusted with the affairs of state, and that he was not the right example for the other ministers and officials to follow. When Yao Jia heard this, he developed a grudge against Han Fei. Yao Jia later slandered Han Fei by saying, "He is a member of the royal family of Han, and he loves his home state and would not help Qin whole-heartedly; he will be a hindrance to Qin's great cause of unification."

The Qin King accepted the two men's suggestion and ordered his men to arrest Han Fei. Li Si secretly had some poison sent to Han Fei and asked him to commit suicide. Han Fei tried in vain to see the king to defend himself, but in failing to gain an audience, he took the poison. Before long, the king regretted his decision, and sent orders to pardon Han Fei. But it was too late; Han Fei was already dead.

For several successive years, the Qin army continued attacking the Zhao State, and had many battles with the best troops of Zhao without paying much attention to Han. During these years, the Han State, weak and small, had to offer Qin its land for an ephemeral peace. Such a peace enabled Han to linger on in a steadily worsening condition for several more years before it came to

韩非到了秦国后，上书秦王说：韩国向秦国称臣，已经有三十多年了，就像是秦国的一个郡县一样。秦国当今最大的对手是赵国。韩国虽小，但如果上下齐心协力，积极备军，固守城池，那么秦国要在短时间内消灭韩国就不太可能。秦军不能大获全胜，只是占一城而退，那么天下之人也就不会听从秦国了。韩国背弃秦国，与赵国、魏国、齐国坚守盟约，那么事情就对秦国不利了。

秦王虽然赏识韩非的才能，但还不能完全信任他，韩非留在秦国也就无所作为。

李斯和韩非是同窗。李斯对秦王说："韩非是韩国的公子，秦国打算吞并诸侯，韩非终究会为韩国着想，这是人之常情。秦国不能任用韩非，如果把他送回韩国，必将是我们的隐患，不如找个借口把他杀了。"

姚贾是魏国的守门人，身份卑贱，曾盗窃，后又遭到赵国的驱逐，声名狼藉（jí），但来到秦国，秦王却很重视他，让他担任重要官职。韩非对秦王说，这样的人怎么可以参与国家大计，这也不是激励群臣的办法。姚贾听说后，怀恨在心，乘机诽谤韩非说："韩非是韩国的王室，心想着韩国，不会真心帮助秦国，留下他只会妨碍秦国的统一大业。"

秦始皇秦王听从了两人的意见，下令拘捕韩非。李斯暗中让人给韩非送去毒药，让他自杀。韩非想面见秦王，表白心迹，却最终没能如愿。后来秦王有些后悔，忙令人赦（shè）免韩非，但韩非已死。

秦军连续数年大举进攻赵国，不断地与赵军的精锐部队交战，根本没有把韩国放在眼里。弱小的韩国用它仅存的土地换来短暂的平静，苟延残喘。秦王十六年（公元前231年），

its end. In 231 B.C. (16 years after King Ying Zheng came to the throne), Han once again offered its land to Qin for peace, even though only a very small piece of land around Luoyang remained of the Han State. The next year, Qin began an attack on Han, and Han collapsed at the first blow of the Qin army, becoming the first state annexed into the Qin Empire. The king of Han was captured, and what had been Han before now became a county of Qin—the county of Yingchuan.

The attack on Han was not a great battle, but strategically it was significant victory because Han's territory directly blocked passage into the North China Plain. By wiping out Han, Qin removed an obstacle on their way to the east. At the same time, the victory also served as a great deterrence to the other states. Now that Qin had the midland of Han, it was able to assemble its troops promptly before it launched any attacks on the other states.

At this time, the Zhao State had a powerful army. Even as Qin was executing its plan to annex Han, its massive military attacks were always focused on Zhao.

The Zhao State, situated in the north and a close neighbor of the Han State, held an important geographic location. The men of Zhao had a natural disposition of being tough and valiant and were very fond of horseback riding and toxophily. As they were frequent victims of the raids of the surrounding powers and northern nomads, such as the Huns, the Zhao State emphasized weapons training. After many years of development, the state had a relatively strong military power. Before King Ying Zheng of Qin came to the throne, the two states of Qin and Zhao had warred often with one another. At the Battle of Changping, more than 400 000 Zhao soldiers were killed. Though Qin had won the victory, it also suffered a disastrous loss. For this reason, Qin always kept a close guard against Zhao.

In 236 B.C. (11 years after King Ying Zheng came to the throne), the Zhao State launched an attack on the Yan State with most of its troops. Qin Shihuang, 23 years old then, decided to take this rare opportunity to launch an attack against Zhao in the name of helping the Yan State. He appointed Wang Jian, a general skilled at art of war, as the commander-in-chief. The Qin army began its attack on Zhao from two directions. Wang Jian and his men took nine Zhao cities, and the land south of the Zhanghe River in Zhao was all occupied by the Qin State.

Thirteen years after King Ying Zheng came to the throne (in 234 B.C.), the Qin State launched another attack on Zhao at Pingyang. The Zhao army was defeated, with 100 000 soldiers dead on the battlefield, including their command-

韩国再次割地求和，献出大片土地给秦国，自己只剩下洛阳周围的一小块地盘。第二年，秦兵攻韩。韩国不堪一击，很快就被攻克了，成为六国中第一个被吞并的诸侯国。韩王做了俘虏，韩国故地成为秦国的一个郡——颍（yǐng）川郡。

秦国灭掉韩国，虽然战役不大，但却是一次重大的战略胜利。秦国由此打开了通向东方的门户，同时，也对其他的诸侯国形成了极大的震慑（shè）。秦国可以凭借韩国所处的地理中央的位置，迅速调集军队，进攻其他的诸侯国。

赵国兵力强盛，秦国在实施灭韩计划的同时，军事打击的重点始终放在赵国。

赵国地处北方，紧邻韩国，地理位置十分重要。当地人生性强悍，喜好骑射，由于受到周边强国和北方匈奴等游牧民族的侵扰，赵国一向重视军备。经过多年的发展，赵国成了一个军事力量比较强大的国家。秦王嬴政即位前，秦、赵之间就有过多次大规模的战争。其中长平大战，赵国损失四十多万大军，秦国虽然取得胜利，但也付出了惨重的代价。因此，秦国对赵国不敢掉以轻心。

秦王十一年（公元前 236 年），赵国率兵攻打燕国。二十三岁的秦始皇毅然决定趁赵国内部空虚，任命善于用兵的将领王翦（jiǎn）为秦军主帅，以救燕国为名，兵分两路进攻赵国。王翦等攻下赵国九城，赵国漳（zhāng）河以南的地区全部被秦国占领。

秦王十三年（公元前234年），秦国进攻赵国的平阳，赵军大败，十万将士战死沙场，连赵军主帅也未能幸免。秦王非常

in-chief. During the battle, the Qin King showed great concern over the situation, and even went to the battlefront in person. The next year, Qin began to attack the northern part of Zhao, and with the support of the troops to the south of the Zhanghe River, the Qin army executed an encirclement around Zhao. They seemed to be determined to wipe out the Zhao State at one fell swoop. At this critical moment, the Zhao King had his general Li Mu sent back from the frontier to stop the Qin attack.

Li Mu was a prominent Zhao general with many achievements in battle and great prestige. For a long time he garrisoned the northern Zhao border to prevent the raids of the Huns. His strategy seemed very conservative— defending instead of attacking. He had many beacon towers built for early-warning against Hun's raid, and with these towers, at the first sign of danger, he could withdraw the residents and their flocks and herds back into the city. He could then order his men to make their defense within the city and not leave to answer the enemy's battlefield challenge. For this reason, in spite of Hun's numerous raids, the Zhao State actually suffered no serious loss. But many people did not quite understand such a strategy of defense. They thought that Li Mu was too timid to fight the Huns. The Zhao King also believed what was said about him and dismissed him from his post, appointing another man to replace him. The new general completely gave up Li Mu's strategy of defense. Whenever the Huns came to raid, he would lead his men out of the city to fight with the enemy. The result was that they were defeated by the Hun's troops many times and suffered great losses. Their people could find no peace on border. This left the king no alternative but to reinstate Li Mu— but Li Mu pretended to be ill and refused to accept the appointment. At the king's repeated requests, Li Mu came to see the king and said, "Since Your Majesty insist on my reinstatement, I will do as you wish, though I will still employ my old strategy. I beg Your Majesty allow me to do so." This time, the king surely accepted his suggestion.

So Li Mu guarded the border with his old strategy. Several years passed, and his soldiers did not fight with the enemy, yet still received munificence from the state. They all felt that they were unworthy of such a treatment, and all hoped could someday fight for their state. Seeing their high morale, Li Mu lost no time in training these soldiers, and prepared extensively for the war. When everything was ready, he decided to incite a battle with the Huns. He scattered many heads of cattle in the steppes, and sent farmers there as decoys. When a small troop of the Huns came, he pretended that he was unable to withstand their attack and retreated. When the Huns heard about this, they at

关注战局，还曾亲临前线。第二年，秦国进攻赵国的北部，与在漳河以南的秦军配合，形成包围之势，大有一举消灭赵国的势头。赵王在危机之中，急忙从边疆调回李牧，阻击秦军。

李牧是赵国的名将，战功显赫，威震四方，长期驻守在赵国北部边境防御匈奴。李牧的战略看起来十分保守，他防御匈奴的策略就是以防守为主。他设立烽火台加以警戒，一旦有匈奴入侵，他总是迅速将居民和牛羊撤回城内，严防死守，并不应战。所以，尽管匈奴多次侵扰边界，但并未造成很大的损失。许多人不理解这种防守战略，以为李牧胆怯，赵王也相信了这种说法，将他撤职，改派他人。新任将军一改李牧的防守策略，匈奴一来就积极迎战，结果多次被匈奴打败，损失很大，边境不得安宁。赵王无奈，只得重新起用李牧。李牧称病不出，赵王一再请求。李牧说："如果大王坚持让我领兵，我还是采用原来以防备为主的办法，请大王允许。"这一次，赵王当然答应。

李牧仍采用老办法守卫边疆。几年过去了，士兵们没有打仗却不停地接受赏赐，都觉得对不住国家，希望拼死一战。李牧看到士气高涨，于是抓紧训练士兵，积极准备作战物资，决定与匈奴大战一场。他派人放出大量的牛马，引诱匈奴。一小股匈奴士兵前来抢夺，赵国军队假装抵挡不住，退败下来。

once sent their forces to attack Zhao. Li Mu immediately had the chariots and crossbowmen defend and hold at the front while the infantry and cavalry enveloped from both flanks, wiping out the invaders. According to historical records, in this battle, the Zhao army "annihilated the 100 000 strong Hun cavalry." After this battle, the Huns did not dare cross the Zhao border for over a decade.

Now the Zhao King appointed Li Mu the general-in-chief and asked him to stop Qin's attack—and Li Mu did not disappoint the king. He led his army to meet the enemy head-on and routed the Qin army. The Zhao army won a full victory, and Li Mu himself was made Lord Wu An by the king.

Two years later, to revenge the failure it had suffered, the Qin army branched out into two columns and launched another fierce attack on Zhao. Once again Li Mu led his army against the enemy. To contend with the main Qin forces, he concentrated the main Zhao forces in the north. At first he ordered his men to remain inactive, and when the enemy troops passed the long and narrow area in the mountain, he ordered his men to make an onslaught on enemy. The Qin army was defeated again. Realizing that he could not conquer Zhao in a short time, the Qin King started to attack the states of Han and Wei.

Sixteen years after the Qin King came to the throne (in 231 B.C.), a great earthquake took place in the northern part of Zhao, which formed a huge crack in the earth of 130 steps long from east to west. To make things even worse, the next year the state was stricken with a famine and the people in Zhao suffered from starvation. Things were just as a folk rhyme of the time described,

"Folks in Zhao are crying,

while those in Qin are laughing.

About this if you have doubts,

see the weeds in the fields."

Because of these natural disasters, the power of the Zhao State had been seriously weakened. But for the Qin King, this was a perfect opportunity for him to attack Zhao. Once again the Qin army branched out into two columns. One column led by General Wang Jian went down to the south via Jingxing— the gateway to Zhao to besiege Handan (the Zhao capital) from the north; another column led by general Yang Duanhe attacked Handan from the south. The Zhao State sent general Li Mu and Sima Shang with their troops to meet the enemy. When the armies of the both states were pitted against each other, they found that they were equally matched.

But Qin determined they would win by any means possible, so they

匈奴闻讯，大举进攻，李牧立刻命令士兵从两边夹击，一举歼灭匈奴入侵者，史书上记载，"杀匈奴十余万骑"。此后十几年，匈奴再也不敢靠近赵国的边境。

此时，赵王任命李牧为大将军，李牧不负重托，率军迎战秦军。秦军溃败，赵军大获全胜，李牧因此被封为武安君。

两年之后，秦军气势汹（xiōng）汹，兵分两路，再次大举进攻赵国，欲报上次失败的耻辱。李牧率军迎敌，并把赵军主力集中在北部，迎战秦军主力。李牧起先按兵不动，等待秦国部队走到山间的狭长地段时，再下令猛攻。秦军再次失败。秦王一时攻不下赵国，便转而攻打韩国和魏国。

秦王十六年（公元前231年），赵国北部发生了大地震，地面裂缝东西长一百三十步。第二年，又遭遇饥荒，人民饱受饥饿之苦。当时民谣说："赵国人在嚎哭，秦国人在大笑。如果不信，但看遍地荒草。"* 赵国国力大为削弱。秦王乘此机会，派兵进攻赵国。秦军分为两路，王翦大军经过赵国北部的门户井陉（xíng）南下，从北面围攻邯郸；杨端和则率兵从南面直攻邯郸。赵国派将军李牧、司马尚分别率军迎敌。两军对垒（lěi），相持不下。

秦国不择手段，运用反间（jiàn）计，派间谍入赵，向赵

---

* 原文："赵为号，秦为笑。以为不信，视地之生毛。"

employed an "estrange stratagem," and Qin sent many spies to the Zhao court. In order to wage distrust between the Zhao King and the two generals, Li Mu and Sima Shang, the spies bribed a key courtier named Guo Kai. When Guo Kai's pocket was sufficiently lined, he tried all he could to impress on the Zhao King that Li Mu's meritorious military service was too illustrious, which made his military power too great, and that he was planning to revolt. Qin's plan succeeded. The Zhao King believed what Guo Kai said and decided to let Zhao Cong and Yan Ju replace Li Mu and Sima Shang. Li Mu considered it improper to give up military leadership while his army was fighting with Qin and refused to hand over the commandership. As a consequence, he was soon arrested and executed on the king's orders, and Sima Shang was also removed from his post. It seems such a bitter irony that Li Mu, such a skilled general, would die a victim of political treachery.

When they heard the news about Li Mu's death, all the members of the Qin army were drinking to cheer this great victory, as the Zhao King had destroyed their greatest enemy with his own hands. With Li Mu's death, the fall of Zhao became inevitable. Three months later, the army led by Wang Jian moved down directly upon Handan. The newly appointed generals Zhao Cong and Yan Ju could not resist their attack, and the army of Zhao was utterly routed at the first encounter with the Qin army. General Zhao Cong was killed, and another general, Yan Ju, fled from the battlefield. Handan was captured and the Zhao King was also taken captive. Zhao had now joined Han's doom at the hands of the Qin King.

After the collapse of the Zhao State, Prince Jia, the elder brother of the Zhao King, escaped to the land of Dai with several hundred men of his clan and made himself King of Dai. He pulled together the people who ran away from Zhao, and this self-made king attached himself to the Yan State and led his people to resist Qin. But his resistance was futile. In 222 B.C., on its way back after the attack on Yan, the Qin army wiped out Dai with little trouble and captured its king.

Now Qin occupied the former lands of Han and Zhao. With this land, the Qin army was placed in a position that enabled it to act on either the offensive or on the defensive, whichever it deemed fit. Qin had extended its power throughout the Yellow River region, and Ying Zheng was now confident that his state would unify China under his rule.

王的宠臣郭开行贿，让他离间赵王与李牧、司马尚的关系。郭开中饱私囊（náng），便对赵王说，李牧战功太大，兵权太盛，有意造反。赵王听信了郭开的话，便让赵葱和颜聚取代李牧。李牧心想：现在正是对秦军作战的关键时刻，赵王怎么能临阵换将呢？他拒绝交出军权。赵王还是逮捕了他，将其处死。可惜李牧一代名将，死都不能瞑（míng）目。司马尚也被免职。

李牧已死，秦军饮酒祝贺。秦国借赵人之手，轻而易举地除掉了劲敌李牧，赵国的末日即将来临。三个月后，王翦率军直扑邯郸，赵国新任命的将军赵葱和颜聚根本不是秦军的对手，赵军一触即溃，赵葱被杀，颜聚逃亡。赵国的京城邯郸被攻破，赵王成了秦军的俘虏，又一个诸侯国覆灭了。

赵亡之后，赵王的哥哥公子嘉带领宗族数百人，逃到了代郡，自立为代王，收拢逃来的赵国人，依附燕国，继续与秦对抗。但此时的代王已经是强弩之末，根本威胁不到秦国了。公元前222年，秦军在消灭燕国回来的途中，不费吹灰之力就攻下了代郡，俘虏了代王嘉。

秦国占领了韩国、赵国，进可以攻，退可以守，此时秦国的势力范围几乎包括了整个黄河流域，统一天下已胜券在握。

荆轲刺秦王

The assassination of Qin Shihuang by Jing Ke

五 图穷而匕首见

Chapter V   The Map Unrolled, the Dagger Revealed

After they captured the Zhao king, the Qin troops marched up to north and were stationed in Zhongshan (the place is the modern day county of Ding in Hebei Province) to make preparations for attacking the Yan State. Their movement threw the whole state of Yan into panic. At this critical time, the Crown Prince of Yan, Prince Dan, plotted the death of the Qin King (the famous scheme of "Jing Ke killing the Qin King").

Prince Dan was the son of King Xi of Yan and had lived for some time in Handan of Zhao as a hostage, much like Ying Zheng's father. Perhaps for this reason, Ying Zheng and Prince Dan had been friends as children. After Ying Zheng came to the throne, Prince Dan came to Qin as a hostage. Prince Dan thought Ying Zheng would give him preferable treatment in Qin, but he was wrong.

Prince Dan lived in Qin for more than 10 years. During this period of time, he harbored resentment against Ying Zheng and missed his home state terribly. When Prince Dan made his request to the Qin King to let him return, the king replied, "You may not go home unless the head of the crow turns white and the horse has horns on its head." Legend had it that upon hearing the reply, Prince Dan's heart was filled with grief and indignation, and he looked up to the sky. Then a miracle happened: The head of a crow really turned white and a horse had horns on its head. This left the Qin King no choice but to keep his words and let Prince Dan return to Yan. But the king set a trap for Prince Dan on his way back to Yan. The king's men damaged a bridge which Prince Dan would surely pass through, so that when Prince Dan walked on the bridge, it would collapse and the prince would die in the accident. But when Prince Dan came near the bridge, a flood dragon carried him across the river and the trap failed. When he came to Hangu Pass, a mountain pass, the gate of the pass was closed, so Prince Dan made a crow call and was echoed by all the cocks nearby. The gate opened and Prince Dan, after experiencing innumerable trials and hardships, reached the Yan State at last.

After he returned to Yan, Prince Dan vowed revenge on Ying Zheng. He said to Ju Wu, his tutor master, "Our state is in the remote area in the north, and it is small in area and weak in power. Therefore, it is impossible for our state to resist Qin with force of arms. I am to gather the heroes all over the country at the expense of the whole of our financial resources. Then we will wait for the opportune moment and have the Qin King assassinated."

But Ju Wu cautioned Prince Dan against vexing Qin out of resentment. He said, "In the west, Yan should ally with the three states of Zhao, Wei and Han; in the south, we should unite with the states of Qi and Chu; and in the north,

秦军俘虏赵王之后，迅速北上，屯兵中山（今河北定县），准备进攻燕国。燕国一片恐慌，危亡之际，燕太子丹亲自筹划了荆轲（jīng kē）刺杀秦王的计划。

燕太子丹是燕王喜的儿子，曾在赵国邯郸做过人质。秦王嬴政的父亲子楚也在赵国做过人质，大约是这个缘故，嬴政年少时就与太子丹相识，而且相处得很好。嬴政即位后，燕太子丹来到秦国做人质。他以为嬴政一定会善待自己，但没想到嬴政对他并不友好。

太子丹在秦国一住就是十多年，心怀愤懑（mèn），希望回国。他向秦王请求，秦王说："如果乌鸦的头变成白色，马长出角来，就准许你回国。"传说，燕太子丹满怀悲愤，仰天长叹。就在此时，乌鸦果然白了头，马头居然生了角。秦王不得已，只得放燕太子丹回国。但又在途中的桥上设有机关，想在太子丹经过时，因桥面倒塌而死。可是，太子丹经过的时候，有蛟龙载着他飞过了桥面，设计的机关没能够启动。到了函谷关，关隘（ài）的大门还没有打开，太子丹就学鸡叫，于是所有的鸡都打鸣，大门开启，太子丹历尽千辛万苦，终于逃出秦国回到燕国。

太子丹回到燕国后，发誓报仇。他对师傅鞠（jū）武说："燕国处在偏僻的北方，力量弱小，无法凭借武力抗击强秦。我决心倾国库的财力，网罗天下的勇士，等待时机，刺杀秦王。"

鞠武不同意太子丹的做法，认为不能以一时的怨气激怒秦国，他说："燕国应在西边联合赵、魏、韩三国，南边团结齐、

we should form an alliance with the Huns. Only in this way can we defeat Qin."

But Prince Dan did not agree with Ju Wu. He said, "Master, your scheme takes time and cannot yield immediate results. I'm afraid that before we have the chance to form any alliances, Yan will be destroyed."

Seeing that nothing could stop Prince Dan from attempting an assassination on the Qin King, Ju Wu recommended him a hero named Tian Guang for the mission. But since Tian Guang was too old to fulfill the task, he introduced Jing Ke to Prince Dan. Tian Guang said, "All the heroes Your Highness have gathered are worthless. But Jing Ke is a born hero, because when he thinks it necessary, he can conceal his pleasure, anger, sorrow, and joy from anyone. He is an excellent swordsman and the perfect man for the mission."

Jing Ke was originally from the Wei State. Being a free-spirited man with brains, courage and insight, Jing Ke loved reading, swordplay and drinking. After traveling from place to place, he came to stay in the Yan State and made friends with two men, a man named Gao Jianli and another man, who was a butcher. Many times people saw them passing the days together drinking and merrymaking. Whenever they were intoxicated, Gao Jianli would play the *zhu** while Jing Ke would sing to the music. When drunken, they would stagger through the busy streets, weeping and laughing loudly as if there were no one else present. But Tian Guang thought highly of Jing Ke and was on good terms with him.

So Prince Dan asked Tian Guang to find Jing Ke for him. He told Tian Guang, "If you can persuade Jing Ke to assassinate the Qin King, you will have saved the Yan State." Prince Dan reminded Tian Guang before Tian left that this was a confidential state affair.

Therefore, Tian Guang went to meet Jing Ke and told him about Prince Dan's scheme. When Jing Ke promised to do all he could to carry out the assassination, Tian Guang said, "Before I came here Prince Dan said to me, 'This is a confidential state affair, so please keep it a secret.' Now my mission is finished." To inspire Jing Ke with courage, Tian killed himself before Jing's eyes.

Soon Prince Dan received Jing Ke in person as his distinguished guest. The prince built Jing Ke a luxurious house by the Yishui River, offered him sumptuous food of all tastes daily, and also presented him numerous rare jewels and precious stones. But a long time passed, and Jing Ke did not make any move to assassinate the Qin King. By then, Qin had already stationed its

楚，北边汇合匈奴，结盟团结，才能够战胜秦国。"

太子丹不赞同："师傅的计谋旷日持久，不是短时间内可以实现的，恐怕到时联合未成，我燕国早已灭亡。"

鞠武见太子丹行刺之意已决，就向他推荐勇士田光。这时候田光的年纪已经很大，无法完成使命。田光于是再向太子丹推荐剑客荆轲，说："太子目前所收罗的勇士没有可用之人。只有荆轲是天生的勇士，喜怒哀乐不表现出来，精于剑术，能当大任。"

荆轲是卫国人，喜欢读书击剑，有谋略，有胆识，是一位慷慨之士。荆轲好饮酒，来到燕国后，常常与好友高渐离和一位屠夫在集市上饮酒。酒酣之时，高渐离击筑（筑，一种乐器），荆轲唱歌，醉行于闹市之中，时而大声痛哭，时而放声大笑，旁若无人。田光欣赏荆轲，待他很好。

燕太子丹拜托田光去请荆轲，说："如果先生可以说服荆轲刺杀秦王，那么燕国就有救了。"田光临行，太子丹嘱咐他说："先生，这是国家大事，请一定保密。"

田光见到荆轲，将太子丹派遣勇士刺杀秦王的计划告诉了他，荆轲答应一定效力。田光又说："太子与我临别时说，这是国家大事，不能泄露，我的任务完成了。"于是在荆轲面前自杀以激励他。

太子丹见到荆轲，把他奉为最尊贵的宾客。在易水河边为荆轲修建了一座豪华住宅，提供丰盛美食和珍奇玩物。但过了很久，荆轲也没有入秦行刺之意。此时，秦军已经驻扎

---

*　*Zhu*: an ancient stringed instrument.

army on Yan's southern border and was waiting for the right time to cross the Yishui River and launch their attack. Prince Dan was terrified, and he urged Jing Ke to make the move as soon as possible. But Jing Ke told the prince that in order to kill the Qin King, he needed to get close to him. "If I went there empty-handed, without anything to present as a gift of trust, the king would not see me. General Fan Wuqi (an ex-general in the Qin army), now living as a refugee in Yan, once offended the Qin King, and the king offered for Fan's head 1 000 *liang* gold plus a title of nobility. In addition, the Qin King has coveted the land of Dukang ❶ in Yan for a long time. If I could present him General Fan's head and the map of Dukang, he would be pleased, and I could come close to him and then attack. This is the only way an assassination would work."

Jing Ke's suggestion troubled Prince Dan. The prince did not have the heart to kill Fan Wuqi and take his head to give the Qin King. It seemed to the prince illogical and unreasonable to kill this general who escaped from his home state and sought refuge in Yan. Seeing Prince Dan's hesitance, Jing Ke paid a visit to Fan Wuqi himself. "General," he said to Fan, "a great deal of animosity exists between you and the Qin State. All the members of your family, young and old, were killed in the name of the state. And now the Qin King has offered 1 000 *liang* gold plus a title of nobility for your head. What do you think of this?"

When he heard this, Fan Wuqi cast his eyes up to the sky and sighed, tears streaming down his cheeks. He said: "Whenever I think on these things, I feel as if a knife were being twisted inside my heart, but there was nothing I could do about it."

Jing Ke said: "I have a scheme with which we can save Yan from destruction and avenge your family as well. Will you hear me out?" Fan Wuqi asked what the scheme was. Jing Ke explained: "If I could present your head to the Qin King, he would be greatly pleased, and would want to meet with me. Once I came close to him, I would seize his sleeve with my left hand and thrust a dagger into his chest with my right hand. Thus you could avenge your family, and Yan would be free of the Qin threat. What do you think of my scheme, General?"

Fan Wuqi rolled up his sleeve, bared his chest, and then said: "That is exactly what I wish. Sir, your words have shown me what I should do." After he spoke these words, Fan Wuqi committed suicide by slitting his own throat.

Then Prince Dan obtained a rare dagger for Jing Ke. The dagger was extremely sharp, and with the poison that they smeared on its blade, a single

在燕国南界，伺（sì）机渡过易水，进攻燕国。太子丹恐惧万分，敦促荆轲尽快入秦。荆轲认为要谋杀秦王，关键是具备可以接近秦王的条件，他说："现在空手入秦，没有信物，恐怕见不到秦王。樊於期（fán wū qī）将军得罪过秦王，现在逃亡在燕国，秦王用千金与万户侯来悬赏他的头颅（lú），而燕国督亢（dū kàng）❶之地，秦王垂涎（xián）已久。如果进献樊将军首级和督亢地图这两个礼物，秦王一定大喜，我就有机会接近他，采取行动。只有这样，行刺计划才会成功。"

太子丹认为拿樊於期的人头作为信物，实在很为难，于情于理他都不忍心杀掉这位投靠燕国的将军。荆轲看出太子丹的心意，于是亲自拜访樊於期，对他说："秦国与将军，可谓深仇大恨。樊家老老少少，都被杀戮（lù）。如今秦王悬千金、赏万户侯求购将军的人头，你有什么想法呢？"

樊於期仰天长叹，顿时泪流满面："我每当想到这些，都心如刀割，但却无计可施。"

荆轲说："我有一计，可以解除燕国兵患，替将军报仇，将军愿意听吗？"樊於期问是什么计策。荆轲说："秦王如果看到将军的头颅，一定会很高兴接见我。那时，我左手抓住他的袖子，右手拿匕首刺进他的胸膛。这样，将军的大仇可报，燕国的危机可除。将军意下如何？"

樊於期挽起胳膊，露出胸膛说："这是我日日夜夜都想做的事情，今日才得到先生的教诲。"于是，自刎（wěn）而死。

太子丹为荆轲预先准备了一把名贵的匕首，锋利异常，又

---

❶ 督亢：燕国的地名。
❶ Dukang: a place in the Yan State.

cut would kill instantly. Prince Dan also commanded a warrior of Yan named Qin Wuyang to go to Qin with Jing Ke as his partner.

Dressed in white clothes and hats, Prince Dan and his trusted followers all went to the bank of the Yishui River to bid Jing Ke farewell. Gao Jianli, Jing Ke's old friend, played the *zhu*, and Jing Ke sang to the music. "Piercing wind, freezing river," he sang. "The hero fords, and he never returns!" He sang with great passion, and his song was so solemn and touching that tears filled the eyes of all present.

When he arrived in Qin, Jing Ke bribed Meng Jia, a minion of the Qin King, to inform the king of some things: that the king's might had so intimidated Prince Dan that he had sent his man to Qin to offer a tribute; that their tribute was Fan Wuqi's head and the map of the land of Dukang; and that the Yan people were willing to become His Majesty's servants.

As Jing Ke had hoped, the Qin King was pleased. He put on his court dress and ordered his men to decorate and prepare his palace in Xianyang. Afterward, ministers and officials of all ranks and descriptions stood in two lines at both sides of the king. The shining halberds in soldiers' hands chilled men's hearts, and the cacophony of clocks and drums was deafening. The king wanted all the people to know that he was about to receive the envoy from Yan.

Jing Ke came with General Fan's head in both hands, followed by Qin Wuyang, who carried the map case. Upon entering the throne room, the stately procession made Qin Wuyang so frightened that his face paled. His behavior aroused the suspicion of the king and his ministers. Turning around, Jing Ke cast a look at Qin Wuyang and gave him a smile. When he came nearer to the king, he apologized for his companion's behavior. "He comes from a small state in the north," he said, "and has never set eyes on such dignity as displayed by Your Majesty, the Son of Heaven. He is unaccustomed to the splendors of your palace. I humbly beg that Your Majesty pardon him." King Ying Zheng pardoned Qin Wuyang's odd behavior, and then bid them present him the map of Dukang. Jing Ke took the map case from Qin Wuyang and went calmly toward the king to hand the map. Then the king excitedly unrolled the scroll— to find a shining dagger concealed within. As quick as lightning, Jing Ke grasped the king's sleeve with his left hand, and plunged the dagger towards the King with his right hand—but the dagger missed. The king jumped to his feet with a start and struggled out of Jing Ke's grasp, tearing his sleeve off as he escaped. In a panic, the king tried to draw his sword, but the blade he wore was a ceremonial weapon, crafted especially long to impress onlookers,

在刃上涂满毒药，见血必死。同时让燕国勇士秦舞阳做荆轲的随从。

太子丹及其亲信身穿白色的衣冠，在易水岸边为荆轲送行。荆轲的朋友高渐离击筑，荆轲伴着音乐歌唱起来："风萧萧兮易水寒，壮士一去兮不复还！"歌声激越悲壮，周围的人都流下了眼泪。

荆轲到了秦国，用重金贿赂秦王的宠臣蒙嘉，通过蒙嘉进言秦王："燕太子丹畏惧大王的神威，进献樊於期的人头和燕国督亢地图，愿意做大王的臣仆。"

秦王听说此事，非常高兴。换上朝服，命人在咸阳宫中摆放装饰，布置一新，百官入列，兵戟（jǐ）森严，钟鼓齐鸣，接见燕国使者。

荆轲捧着装有樊於期头颅的盒子，秦舞阳捧着装地图的盒子，走进秦宫大殿。秦舞阳被这威严的气势所震慑，恐惧万分，脸色苍白。站立在大殿两侧的文武群臣都觉得很诧（chà）异。荆轲回头看了秦舞阳一眼，微微一笑，走向前致歉说："他来自北方小国，没见过天子的威仪，希望大王原谅。"嬴政没有怪罪，让荆轲献上燕国督亢之地的地图。荆轲从秦舞阳手中接过地图，从容上前奉上。秦王欣然打开地图，等到全部打开时，露出了一把雪亮的匕首——图穷而匕首见（xiàn，同"现"）。只见荆轲猛地用左手抓住秦王衣袖，右手拿起匕首直刺秦王，但没有刺中。秦王大吃一惊，奋力挣脱，袖子竟被荆轲扯断。嬴政仓皇拔剑，可是剑很长，他拿着剑鞘（qiào），慌乱之中

and its length prevented the king from unsheathing it in haste. Jing Ke pursued the king around one of the columns in the audience hall, and all of the ministers and officials present were too shocked to react against Jing Ke.

According to Qin law, ministers and officials were forbidden to carry any weapons with them when they came to see the king in the audience hall. Even the king's armed guards could only stand at a great distance outside the hall, and were prohibited from entering the hall without orders—and the king was in no state of mind to order them in. At this critical moment, as the king was taking cover behind a pillar, a court doctor named Xia Wuqie threw his medicine bag at Jing Ke to distract him. But the terrified king still could not draw his sword out of its sheath. Then his ministers and officials shouted, "King, shift your sword onto your back!" Their advice helped him come to his senses, and he pushed his sword onto his back and drew it out at last, after which he attacked Jing Ke and cut off Jing's left leg. Seriously wounded, Jing Ke threw the dagger at the king with all of his might, but missed again, instead plunging the dagger into a bronze column. The king stabbed Jing Ke with his sword eight times, and Jing Ke, knowing that his chance was slipping away, leaned against a column and burst into laughter. "I would have killed you," he said, "had I not intended to capture you alive so that I could repay Prince Dan for his kindness to me." Soon after, the armed guards arrived and finished off the assassin.

It took a while before the frightened Qin King calmed down, but once he had, he rewarded the ministers and officials present. While he was doing so, the king praised his court doctor, "Xia Wuqie is truly loyal to me. He was the only man with the presence of mind to do something to counter Jing Ke's attack."

The Qin King was furious at this assassination attempt, so he sent troops to attack Yan with Wang Jian as the commander-in-chief. The Yan army, joined by the forces of Prince Jia, an escaped Zhao leader from the county of Dai, began to counterattack. But the Qin army swept the area west of the Yishui River, and in 226 B.C., the army led by Wang Jian captured the the city of Ji, the Yan capital (the modern Beijing). The Yan King and his son, Prince Dan, escaped to Liaodong (around the present city of Liaoyang in Liaoning Province) with the remnants of their forces. But Li Xin, a general in the Qin army, led his forces in pursuit. Then King Jia of Dai suggested that the Yan King kill Prince Dan. He said that the person the Qin King hated the most was Prince Dan, and if the Yan King killed Prince Dan, Qin would withdraw its army and Yan would not be destroyed. The fearful king proceeded to kill his

根本拔不出剑来。荆轲追逼秦王，秦王围着大殿当中的立柱乱跑。群臣都惊呆了，完全不知所措。

按照秦国的法规，群臣上殿不准携带任何武器；卫士手持兵器立于殿下，没有命令不准上殿。情急之中，秦王根本来不及招呼士兵上殿护卫。一位御医名叫夏无且，将随身带着的药囊砸向荆轲。嬴政绕着柱子奔跑躲避，惊恐万分，根本不知道如何是好。群臣大声呼喊："王负剑！"秦王的剑很长，不能一下子拔出剑鞘，如果把剑推到背后，则容易拔出。秦王醒悟，将剑置于背后，拔出长剑，直刺荆轲，砍断了他的左腿。荆轲身负重伤，于是奋力用匕首掷向秦王，没有击中，匕首刺入铜柱。嬴政连砍荆轲八剑，荆轲自知已经失败，靠在柱子上大笑："今天之所以没有成功，是想生擒（qín）你，以报答太子丹。"此时，左右卫士上前，杀了荆轲。

秦王受到惊吓，过了很久才缓过神来。不久，秦王赏赐在场的官员，感叹道："还是夏无且对我忠诚，知道用药囊砸荆轲。"

遭遇燕国的刺客行刺，秦王大怒，立即派兵，任命王翦统帅大军，全力伐燕。燕国联合逃到代郡的赵国公子嘉，合力反击。秦军在易水以西的地方大获全胜。公元前226年，王翦率军攻占了燕国的都城蓟（jì）城（今北京市）。燕王和太子丹率领残余部队逃往辽东（今辽宁省辽阳市一带），秦将李信穷追不舍。代王嘉劝燕王说，秦王痛恨的是太子丹，如果燕王杀死太子丹则可以使秦国退兵，燕国不亡。燕王被迫将太子

own son and give his head to the Qin King, hoping for the forgiveness. But the Qin forces continued their attack.

In 222 B.C., after Qin absorbed the Chu State, General Wang Ben took a massive army out of Chu to assault Liaodong, capturing the Yan King and finally ending the Yan State.

If Jing Ke had succeeded in his assassination, then that period of Chinese history would have been vastly different. But we will never know for sure. Different people have varying opinions of Jing Ke, but his example of courage has inspired the Chinese for generations.

丹人头献给秦国，以求宽恕。秦国并不领情，仍然进军攻击。

公元前222年，秦国灭楚以后，派王贲（bēn）统帅重兵攻取辽东，俘虏燕王。燕国最终灭亡。

当年荆轲如果行刺成功，那么，这一段历史就得重写。可是，历史从没有第二种选择。不论人们怎样看待行刺，却没有人不被荆轲无畏的勇气所打动。正是非凡的勇敢，使荆轲刺秦王的故事在中国广为流传。

秦陵出土的铜车马

The bronze chariots and horses unearthed
in Qin Shihuang's mausoleum

六　决战齐楚

Chapter Ⅵ　Decisive Battles with the States of Qi and Chu

The Chu State, situated in the middle reaches of the Yangtze River, was a powerful political force during the Spring and Autumn Period. During the Warring States Period, Chu had developed into a vast territory with great influence. But while the Qin State was carrying out various reforms and rising in power, the Chu State was suffering severe setbacks in political, military, and diplomatic affairs. As a result, the state lost its dominant position among the seven states of this period.

In 226 B.C., 21 years after he came to the throne, the Qin King sent his troops to launch an attack on the Chu State. While his intention was a tentative strike to test their defenses, his forces ended up capturing over 10 of the Chu cities. As a result of these quick victories, the Qin King began to believe that the Chu State's soldiers were weak, and their generals incompetent, and he decided that now was the time to finish the Chu State and absorb it into his empire. "In your estimation, General," he asked Li Xin, one of his young generals, "how many men would you need to annex the Chu State?" Li Xin was a courageous and resolute general who had led a troop of more than a thousand soldiers in pursuit of Prince Dan, and had finally been the one to present Prince Dan's head to the Qin King.

"I would only need 200 000 men to take Chu," Li Xin replied.

Then the Qin King asked Wang Jian, his older general, the same question.

"To annex Chu, I would need at least 600 000 men," Wang Jian replied.

Due to his army's many victories, the king was shocked at Wang Jian's words. He said, "General Wang, you have become timid in your old age. General Li is young and courageous, and I trust that his assessment was more correct." So he appointed Li Xin chief general to lead 200 000 men to attack Chu. Wang Jian, claiming ill health, returned to his hometown of Pinyang (the present county of Fuping in Shaanxi Province) to live out his life in retirement.

Li Xin divided his men into two armies and attacked the Chu army from two directions. The two armies formed a junction at Chengfu (the present county of Baofeng in Henan Province), gaining a great initial victory over the Chu army. Then the Chu King appointed Xiang Yan his chief general and ordered him to lead an army of 200 000 men to meet the enemy head-on. Confident in his force's strength, Li Xin did not try to evade the retaliatory strike, and instead he ordered his troops to fight a fierce battle with the main force of the Chu army. Soon the tides turned against Qin, and Li Xin's army was forced to retreat. The Chu army continued pursuing the fleeing Qin forces for three days until they caught them, scattering the defeated Qin army.

When the news of Li Xin's failure reached Xianyang, the Qin King was

楚国地处长江中游，春秋时期一度称霸。战国时期，楚国已经发展成为幅员辽阔、国力雄厚的大国。就在秦国不断实行改革，迅速崛起的时期，楚国却在政治、军事和外交上一再失利，导致它在七雄逐鹿的竞争中失去了原有的优势地位。

秦王二十一年（公元前 226 年），秦王派兵向楚国发起试探性的进攻，结果一下子夺取了十几座城池。秦王认为，对手已是兵弱将寡，决定乘势灭楚。他问年轻的将军李信："将军估计一下，要夺取楚国，总共需要多少兵力才足够？"李信勇猛果敢，曾经率领千余人追击燕太子丹，最后献上太子丹的头颅，秦王十分赏识他。

李信回答："不过用二十万。"

秦王又问老将王翦需要多少兵马。

王翦说："非六十万人不可。"

此时的秦王被接连不断的胜利冲昏了头脑，说："王将军确实老了，为何如此胆怯？李将军果敢壮勇，说得对。"于是任命李信为大将，率领二十万人伐楚。王翦自称生病，回老家频阳（今陕西省富平县）养老去了。

起初，李信部队兵分两路，大破楚军，最后会合于城父（今河南省宝丰县）。楚王急忙任命项燕为大将，率兵二十万迎战。李信依仗自己的勇气，不避锋芒，与项燕主力展开激战，秦军不利，楚军穷追不舍，连续追了三天三夜，终于大破李信军队，七名副将战死。秦军仓皇逃走。

李信失败的消息传到咸阳，秦王勃然大怒，后悔没有听王

wroth, and regretted rejecting Wang Jian's advice. So the king went to Pinyang, Wang Jian's hometown, in person and apologized to him. "I failed to heed your words, General," he said, "thus causing our humiliating defeat and sullying the honor of our army. I have heard reports that the Chu army is even now running westward and preparing to launch attack against us. General, I know you are in poor health, but you have always been a kind and loyal subject, and not the type to leave your king in a hopeless situation. Will you help me?"

Wang Jian replied, "I'm old and in poor health, Your Majesty, and my mind isn't as sharp as it used to be. You should choose a better man as your chief general."

But the king did not relent. "You are the only person who can lead our army to attack Chu."

"If you insist on my commanding the armies, Your Majesty," he said, "I will need 600 000 men, no less."

An army of 600 000 men meant the entire armed force of Qin, including the troops that garrisoned Xianyang, the Qin capital. Such a thing never happened before. But the Qin King was resolute in his determination to unify the seven states, so he approved Wang Jian's request.

Soon Wang Jian and his enormous army of 600 000 men were ready to leave Xianyang to repulse the Chu forces. The Qin King went to see them off in person and accompanied them all the way to the place of Bashang. Before they parted, Wang Jian asked the king for large fertile land and fine houses if he returned victorious. The king said, "General, you may go with your mind at rest. Are you afraid that you will live in poverty?" "As a general of Your Majesty," said Wang Jian, "it is impossible for me to rise to the power of a marquis, no matter what I achieve in battle. Like ministers before, I am only asking for this so that I can leave property for my children." Upon hearing this, the Qin King laughed, and promised he would do as Wang Jian wished.

So Wang Jian led his army away. But before they arrived at Hangu Pass, he sent heralds to the king five times, and each time he repeated his request for land and houses. "General," someone said to him, "even if you are begging from the king, you have gone too far."

Wang Jian replied, "Things are not as they seem. Our king is a cruel and willful man. Now that all know he has placed his entire army in my hands, how can he remain unworried? I wish to remind him that I am leading this army because I expect him to grant me property for my children in return, and not for any other purpose. If he knows my motivations, then he will not

翦的话。秦王亲自奔赴王翦老家频阳，向王翦道歉："寡人因为没有听将军的话，致使秦军蒙受耻辱，有损威望。听说楚军连日西进，准备进攻秦国，将军虽然有病，难道真的忍心抛弃寡人吗？""寡人"为君主自称。

王翦说："老臣身体不好，脑子也糊涂了，大王还是另选有才能的将领吧！"

"这次征伐楚国，一定要请将军带兵才行，请不要再推辞了。"

"大王一定要用臣，那么，非六十万兵力不可。"

六十万兵力，等于连同首都咸阳城内的军队也都调走。这是前所未有的事。秦王志在一统天下，完全答应了王翦的要求。

王翦率领六十万大军浩浩荡荡离开咸阳，秦始皇亲自送行，一直送到灞（bà）上。临行前，王翦请求秦王赏赐良田美宅，而且数量很多。秦王说："将军放心走吧，难道还担心受穷吗？"王翦说："作为大王的将军，即使有战功，也不得封侯，以往的大臣，都是请求赏赐田宅，好为子孙留作产业。"秦王听罢，开怀大笑，答应了王翦。

王翦率军前行，到函谷关之前，又连续五次派使者向秦王恳求赐予良田。有人对他说："将军就是向大王乞讨，这样做也很过分了。"

王翦意味深长地说："不是你说的那样。秦王粗暴刚愎（bì），不相信他人，如今几乎是把秦国全部军队都交给我，他能不顾虑重重吗？我这样做是让秦王相信，我只是想为子孙后

distrust me." As an outstanding general, Wang Jian not only knew well the art of war, he also knew how to deal with a king.

To set Wang Jian's heart at rest, the Qin King betrothed Princess Xinyang, his own daughter, to him, despite that Wang Jian was already over 60 while the princess was only at her twenties. The king sent an honor guard to escort the princess to meet Wang Jian. By his orders, the wedding proceeded as soon as they caught up with General Wang. After the wedding, Wang Jian continued to lead his army forward. The place where they were married was renamed Xinyang (the present city of Xinyang in Henan Province).

Facing the great Qin army, the Chu State gathered all its forces to fight against them.

Wang Jian did not attack immediately. Instead, he ordered his army to strengthen their defenses and stay alert. He had them rest and train daily so that they could conserve strength and energy. He improved the soldiers' rations, and would often walk among his men to soothe them, and even eat meals with them. The Chu army threw down the proverbial gauntlet in challenge several times, but each time the Qin army refused to leave their camps to pick it up. After some time, Wang Jian asked his men which games they were playing in camp. They said that they had organized competitions that involved seeing who could fling heavy stones the farthest, and who could jump the farthest. Wang Jian was pleased to hear this, as he figured his men's morale was high, and that now was the right time to make their attack. Since they had failed to bait out the Qin army, the Chu soldiers were exhausted and demoralized, and they had begun breaking camp to retreat. But before they could flee, Wang Jian led his elite troops in a surprise attack, pursuing the Chu army and finally defeating them at Qinan (in modern Su County in Anhui Province). Over the course of these battles, Xiang Yan, the chief general of the Chu army, was killed. The Qin army continued its triumphant rout, taking many cities and capturing much of the Chu State's land. A year later, Wang Jian and his army marched into the Chu capital and captured its king, setting up new administrative divisions in the captured land. After Chu was completely absorbed into the Qin Empire, Wang Jian led his army south and subjugated the Yue State, a lesser state dependent on Chu. In only a little over a year, Wang Jian conquered the entire Chu State and annexed it as Qin territory.

Twenty-two years after the Qin King came to the throne (in 225 B.C.), Wang Ben, another Qin general, began an attack on the Wei State. Since the city walls of the Daliang, the Wei capital, were tall and strong, the Qin army attacked

代多留些财产，别无他意，这样秦王就不会怀疑我了。"作为一位杰出的将军，王翦深知如何与君主周旋。

为了使王翦安心，就在王翦行军的路上，秦始皇把芳龄二十多岁的信阳公主许配给年逾花甲的王翦，并派一支军队护送信阳公主，规定在哪里追上王将军，就在哪里结婚。公主很快赶上王翦，匆匆结了婚，王翦又率大军继续前进。后来，他们结婚的地方，便取名为信阳（今河南省信阳市）。

楚国听说王翦率领重兵前来，于是调集国中所有的军队抵抗秦军。

王翦令军队坚壁守卫，休息操练，养精蓄锐，改善饮食，抚慰将士，他还亲自与士卒一道吃饭。楚军多次挑战，秦军都不出营应战。过了一段时间，王翦问军中都在玩什么游戏，部下回答："士兵们正在比赛扔巨石和跳远呢。"王翦十分高兴，认为此时士气高扬，可以出战了。楚军因多次挑战而疲惫不堪，士气低落，开始撤营退却。王翦于是率领精锐部队为前锋，全线追击，在蕲南（今安徽省宿县）大败楚军，杀了楚军统帅项燕。秦军乘胜追击，攻城略地。大约一年时间，就俘虏了楚王，在楚国的故地设置新的行政郡县。灭楚以后，王翦率军继续南下，征服了附属于楚国的越国。仅用一年多的时间，王翦就将楚国划入秦国的版图之中。

秦王二十二年（公元前225年），秦将王贲开始攻打魏国，魏国都城大梁城墙高大坚固，秦军采用水攻，引黄河水淹没大

the city by flooding it with water from the Yellow River. Eventually, the walls collapsed from the pressure of the flood. The Wei King then surrendered to his Qin conquerors, but the Qin King still had the Wei King killed, sending his armies into Wei and absorbing the state into his empire.

By 222 B.C., the 25th year of his reign, the Qin King had annexed the five states of Han, Zhao, Wei, Yan and Chu. The king and his people celebrated these great victories with reveling and merrymaking. Now there was only one state left to conquer: the Qi State, which for many years had remained aloof from the quarrels of the other states.

The Qi State was situated in the Shandong Peninsula. During the Spring and Autumn Period, King Huan of Qi appointed Guan Zhong to reform state policies, and his success in regulating state affairs allowed for the state's rapid development, making it into a great regional power. During the Warring States Period, several generations of Qi kings continued using Guan Zhong's successful policies, and promoted the state's continued development. For this reason, the Qi State became a rich and powerful state with a much developed culture. The state set up an institute of learning in a place called Jixia, which later became a center for academic pursuits, and where people freely exchanged ideas and scholars held debates and gave lectures. For some time, the two states of Qi and Qin remained powerful opposing forces, one in the east and the other in the west.

In the late Warring States Period, seeing the wars that ravaged the other states, the Qi State observed a general principle of neutrality, and for more than 40 years it stayed out of these conflicts. During the battle of Changping between Qin and Zhao, Zhao tried to seek help from Qi. A minister named Zhou Zili advocated lending support to Zhao. He said, "The Zhao State serves as a barrier between our state and Qin. If we lose this barrier, then before long the states of Qi and Chu would be under the threat of Qin's armies." But the Qi King at the time did not approve of Zhou's proposal.

During the time of King Jian of Qi, a man named Hou Sheng held the position of prime minister of Qi, the highest official in the state. The Qin State sent spies to Qi to bribe Hou Sheng with a great quantity of gold. They also bribed those people of Qi who lived in Qin or traveled to Qin, and those who did business in Qin. Those bribed took every opportunity to persuade the king of Qi to keep a friendly relationship with Qin, to stop any preparations for war, and to refrain from helping any of the other five states in their fights to resist Qin.

The Qi King lacked strategic foresight, and not only did he refuse to

梁城。时间一长，城墙毁坏，魏王投降，但还是被杀，秦军灭魏，占领魏国整个地盘。

秦王二十五年（公元前 222 年），秦王吞并韩、赵、魏、燕、楚五国，为了庆祝这一胜利，秦王恩准天下臣民饮酒欢乐，举行庆祝活动。此时，只剩下偏安一隅（yǔ）的齐国了。

齐国位于山东半岛。春秋时期，齐桓（huán）公任用管仲进行改革，加速了发展的步伐，使齐国成为一个强大的诸侯国。战国时期，齐国的君主继续推行改革，重视发展，国力不断强盛，文化发达。齐国在稷（jì）下这个地方设有学宫，成为当时思想学术交流的中心，许多学者都在这里辩论讲学。齐国一度成为与秦国东西对峙的两大强国。

随后的齐国对各国间的征战大多采取中立的原则，四十多年没有介入过一场战役。秦、赵长平大战时，赵国曾请求齐国帮助。齐国谋臣周子力主张救赵，他说："如果失去赵国的屏障（píng zhàng），用不了多久，齐国和楚国就会受到秦国的威胁。"但当时的君主并没有采纳他的意见。

齐王建的时代，有一位叫后胜的大臣担任相国，即最高执政官。秦国于是派间谍以重金贿赂后胜，也贿赂到秦国游历的齐国士人。受到贿赂的人，一有机会就劝齐王与秦国保持友好关系，停止战备，不要帮助其他五国攻秦。

齐王缺乏战略远见，不仅不能援助五国抗秦，自己也没有

support any of the other five states against Qin, but also failed to prepare his state for war. In 221 B.C., after Wang Ben and his armies absorbed the Yan State, he led his army south—where they could launch an attack on Qi at any time.

When the attacking army had reached the gates of the Qi capital, some officials, led by Hou Sheng, urged the king to surrender, while other officials, led by Yong Men, the minister of war, and Ji Mo, a senior official, advocated enlisting the remaining forces of the other five states to fight Qin. But the king leaned toward capitulating to Qin. Yong Men asked, "What use is a king to the people of his state? Is his purpose to provide lasting stability and enduring peace, or simply to be a figurehead of empty authority?"

"To provide the people of the state with lasting peace and enduring stability," the king replied.

"Since our state already has a king," Yong Men asked, "why should Your Majesty relinquish the state and surrender to Qin?" His words rendered the king speechless, and the king shut himself in his palace.

But the Qi State's military was not strong enough to oppose the invading Qin forces. Since the people who had taken Qin bribes had gained the upper hand in Qi, and since the state was poorly prepared for war, they were unable to mobilize in time. The Qin army then pushed straight into Linzi, the Qi capital, without encountering significant resistance.

To convince the Qi King to surrender, the Qin King promised to grant him a large portion of land of 500 miles if he would abdicate the throne and serve Qin. As King Jian realized he could not resist the Qin forces, he had no choice but to surrender. However, despite the Qin King's promises, he did not grant King Jian the lands he had promised, and instead confined King Jian to a place called "Gong" and starved him to death in a forest of pines and cypresses.

After King Jian's death, the Qi State was absorbed into Qin, and China turned a new page in history as the Qin State achieved complete unification of the seven states.

充分的战前准备。公元前 221 年，秦将王贲统帅的大军在灭燕后南下，随时准备向齐国发起攻击。

兵临城下，齐国后胜等官员竭力劝说齐王投降，雍门司马、即墨大夫等人主张齐王积极联合其他五国残存的力量抵抗秦兵。齐王准备投降，雍门司马说："请问大王，在一国之中设立一个君王，是为了国家的长治久安，还是为了君王自己？"

齐王说："是为了国家的长治久安。"

"既然是为了国家才立王，那么，大王为何要抛弃齐国去投降秦国？"齐王一时无言，只好回宫。

但齐国确实没有军事实力来对抗秦军。由于齐国内部亲秦势力占据上风，齐国准备不足，军民也得不到有效的组织，秦军长驱直入，没有受到多少抵抗就占领了齐国都城临淄（zī）。

为了劝诱齐王投降，秦王曾答应给齐王五百里土地作为他的封地。齐王见大势已去，宣布投降。但秦国把齐王安置在一个叫"共"的地方，将他活活饿死在松柏林子里。

最后一个诸侯国——齐国覆灭了，天下统一，历史开始了新的篇章。

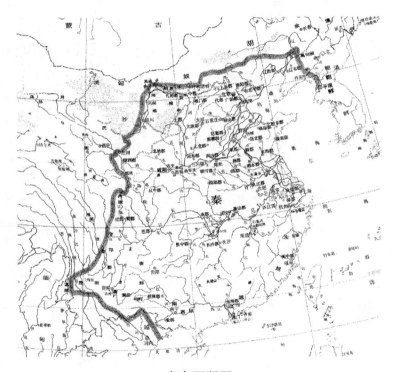

秦帝国版图

Map of the Qin Empire

七 帝国的鸿业

Chapter Ⅶ　Achievements of the Empire

The Spring and Autumn Period was characterized by great turbulence and strife that lasted over 500 years. This turbulence did not end until the Qin State unified China by annexing the other six states.

Now the Qin State had transformed. It had become a great empire with vast territory and hegemonic power. One day, the Qin King said to his ministers and officials, "I owe my success to the blessing of my ancestors. Now the six states have received their due punishment and I have brought order to the country. Unless we establish a title for this dynasty, then future generations will not know of our heroic exploits." He then asked his ministers and officials to discuss what title he should take for himself.

Prime Minister Wang Wan (the highest official in the state), Vice-Prime Minister Feng Jie (in charge of supervising officials) and Li Si (the highest law officer) held a meeting with various other officials to discuss the new title for the king. During their discussion, some said, "In the past, the area that the Five Huangs* ruled was only about 1 000 square *li*. Some of the other local powers paid yearly tribute to these emperors, but others did not recognize their authority at all. And these emperors, though they were sons of Heaven, were powerless to bring these independent powers under control. But as of now, His Majesty the Qin King and his armies have subjected all independent powers to Qin's will, bringing peace back to our land. The land within four seas has become prefectures and counties of the Qin State, and for the first time we have unified laws and decrees, an exploit unheard of since ancient times. The exploits of our king have even exceeded those of the Five Huangs. In ancient times, there were Huang of Heaven, Huang of Earth, and Huang of Tai, among which the Huang of Tai was most respected. So we propose that His Majesty take the title 'Huang of Tai,' and that his order be called 'Zhi,' his proclamation, 'Zhao.' His Majesty, the son of Heaven, should call himself 'Zheng.' "

Upon hearing their proposal, Ying Zheng the Qin King said, "I will only keep 'Huang' in my title. I will, however, add 'Di,' the title for the ancient sovereign, to my new title, and thus call myself 'Huangdi.' " He also created a new title—"Taishanghuang" (super-sovereign) for Zichu, his late father.

Again, the king said: "I'll be the Shi Huangdi*, and my successors will be the Second, Third, and so on forever."

The titles "Huang" and "Di" had been employed long before Qin Shihuang. In ancient times, five legendary emperors ruled over China: Fu Xi, Shen Nong, Huang Di, Yao and Shun. They were called "San Huang (three previous sovereigns)" and "Wu Di (five previous emperors)." But now, with

春秋战国，中国社会经历了五百多年的动荡，直至公元前221 年，秦国吞并六国，完成天下统一。

秦国已经不再是原来的秦国，而是一个面积辽阔、实力雄厚的帝国。秦王说："寡人取得成功，完全依赖先祖神灵的保佑。如今六国之王都得到了应有的惩罚，天下大定。如果名号不改，则不能颂扬功绩，流传后世。"因此，秦王请大臣们商议帝号。

丞相（最高执政官）王绾（wǎn）、御史大夫（负责监察百官）冯劫（jié）、廷尉（负责司法）李斯等召集百官商讨，为秦王取一个新的名号。商量结果，他们说："远古时期的五位帝王所统治的地方，不过方圆千里，而统治中心以外的地方势力，有的来朝拜，有的则不尊，天子不能够完全控制他们。现在，陛下兴起正义之师，诛灭凶残势力，使天下得以平定，四海之内都成了秦国的郡县，法令得到统一。这是上古以来从未有过的事情，五帝的功业也比不上。古代有天皇、地皇、泰皇，泰皇最尊贵，我们提议陛下的尊号是'泰皇'，所宣布的政令称为'制'，所颁发的文告称为'诏'，天子自称'朕'。"

秦王嬴政说："去掉'泰'字，留下'皇'字，再采用上古'帝'的位号，称'皇帝'。"秦王的父亲子楚被称为"太上皇"。

秦王又说："我为始皇帝，后来的继承者用数字为名号，二世、三世至于万世，传之无穷。"

"皇"与"帝"二字在秦始皇之前已有使用。中国远古有五位帝王，伏羲（xī）、神农、黄帝、尧、舜，人们称之为"三皇五帝"。可是，当秦王看着浩浩荡荡的秦军征服整个神州

---

*   the Five Huangs: an address for the Three Sovereigns and Five Emperors, who were legendary emperors or sovereigns in ancient China.

*   Shi Huangdi: the first Huangdi or the first emperor, which is generally known as in Chinese history.

his mighty and numerous armies, the Qin King had conquered the entire Divine Land of China—and all of the other kings and lords, regardless of their influence, had now submitted themselves to him. As a result, the king felt that he possessed all the virtues and powers of "San Huang," and that his achievements had surpassed those of "Wu Di." In his new title, the word "Shi" means "the first," and combined with "Huangdi," the given names of his predecessors, the title "Shi Huangdi" signifies his supremacy over them. He expected that his great empire would be handed down to his descendants, generation after generation, without end. As he was the first emperor of the Qin Dynasty, historians generally call him Qin Shihuang.

A new state pattern had to be developed in the Qin Empire, as no system in China's history could be used for reference, and although Qin Shihuang was a brilliant ruler, his governance and policies can seem somewhat immature. Standing on the summit of China's history, this unique king endowed his empire with a unique fate. Contrary to his expectations, the empire itself did not last forever, but its political system survived in various ways, significantly influencing China's government for more than two millennia afterward.

But conquering the other states by force did not prove that a new dynasty would be established. Without a mystical justification for the unification of China under the Qin, the newly established empire would likely be subverted again by force. All of the previous rulers found various reasons to prove that God's will had established their dynasties. The Shang Dynasty eliminated the Xia Dynasty under this pretext. It is said that when King Wu of Zhou went on a punitive expedition against King Zhou of the Shang Dynasty, some ministers of Shang said, "It is God's will that the Shang Dynasty come to its end." Later, others held that the establishment of the Zhou Dynasty was by the will of God. This divine will could not be resisted, and human power could do nothing about it. In ancient times, human knowledge about nature was very limited, and a primitive religion prevailed, thus meaning that divine will and fatalist ideas could provide adequate explanation for the legitimacy of a dynasty.

After unifying China and setting up the Qin Dynasty, Qin Shihuang tried to establish his position as a legitimate ruler with the theory of " Wu De* Zhong Shi (cycle of the five virtues)" , which was very popular at that time.

During the Warring States Period, scholars emphasized the theory of Yin

大地，看着无论多么显赫的诸侯，全都臣服在自己的仪仗之下时，他确实有充分的理由相信自己是"德兼三皇，功过五帝"。他想象着自己开创的帝国功业，不仅能够在他的手中开始，而且还能够传承二世、三世，直至万世，流传永远。

这位神武圣明的帝王的个性中混合某种"天真"。这种天真源于秦帝国完全是一种新的国家样式，此前的历史没有任何可以借鉴的内容。站在巅（diān）峰之上，秦王很自然地赋（fù）予了帝国独特的命运。秦帝国的命运确实独一无二。当然，秦帝国的统治并没有像嬴政想象的那样传于万世，但帝国政治体制的样式却以各种形式保存下来，对此后两千多年的历史发生了深远的影响。

仅仅依靠武力征服而统一天下，并不能说明王朝的建立具有某种"必然性"。如果缺乏这种"必然性"的证明，那么新建王朝实际上就有再被武力颠覆的可能。秦以前的朝代，都曾为自己王朝的建立寻找种种理由。商汤消灭夏朝，便称这是上天的意志。当周武王征伐商纣（zhòu）王时，商朝的大臣说："上天要结束商朝的命运啊。"当时人认为，周王朝的建立也顺应了天命。天命是人的意志无法抗拒的力量。古代对于自然的认识十分有限，原始宗教流行，因此上天的意志、天命等观念确实能够为王朝的建立提供必然性、合法性的基础。

秦始皇统一天下，建立秦王朝之后，借助当时流行的"五德终始"学说，确立自己正统的地位。

战国时期的阴阳家热衷于谈论阴阳、"五行"学说，后来

---

* *Wu De*: Wu means "five" and De means "virtue," but for the ruling class De actually means power.

and Yang*, and later, other scholars explained changes in the dynasties by employing the *Wu Xing** theory. The so-called *Wu Xing* refers to five elements, water, fire, metal, wood and earth, each representing a particular power, so they are also regarded as the "Five Powers." The generation cycle of the Five Powers is: Wood generates fire, fire generates earth, earth generates metal, metal generates water, and water, in turn, generates wood. "Generate" in this context means to give rise to something, or help something ripen for change. A restriction or conquering relationship also exists among the Five Powers. The conquest cycle of the Five Powers is: Water restricts fire, fire restricts metal, metal restricts wood, wood restricts earth, and earth, in turn, restricts water. "Restrict" in this context means to curb or conquer. Every element in *Wu Xing* corresponds to one kind of "De (virtue)" ; hence, *Wu Xing* to *Wu De*. Every "De" stands for a particular period of reign. The period of the original Huang Di was ruled by the power of earth. Huang Di's reign was replaced by the Xia Dynasty, which ruled by the power of wood. The Xia Dynasty was followed by the Shang Dynasty, which ruled by the power of metal. And the Shang Dynasty was replaced by the Zhou Dynasty, which ruled by the power of fire. Now that the Qin Dynasty had replaced the Zhou, then according to the circulation theory of the five elements, Qin's power of water had overcome Zhou's power of fire. This theory of the generation and restriction of the five elements is partly based on actual human experience. For example, fire can burn wood, and wood generates fire—and when fire is burning, it can be extinguished by water. The ancient people viewed the relationship of these five elements as objective law and they held that just like the circulation of *Wu De*, the changes of dynasties were independent of man's own will, and were inevitable. In this theory the Qin Dynasty did find sufficient legitimacy for its rise to power.

But if the Qin Dynasty used the idea that it was the water that extinguished the fire of the past dynasty, then what evidence could it provide to validate this claim? According to legend, King Wen of Qin, Qin Shihuang's forefather, once captured a black dragon while he was hunting, which was recognized as an omen of gaining the power of water. This auspicious sign allegedly appeared 500 years before the rise of the Qin Dynasty; therefore, as the power of water overcame the power of fire, it could be seen as natural and inevitable that the Qin Dynasty would replace the Zhou Dynasty. Since the new dynasty represented the power of water, it should govern according to the pattern of water, with black as its symbolic color and six as its lucky number. At the advent of Qin Shihuang's rule, he changed the name of the Heshui

的学者又运用"五行"来解释历代王朝更替的现象。"五行"指水、火、金、木、土等五种物质。"五行"之间的关系是：木生火，火生土，土生金，金生水。"生"有生成、形成，具备生成条件的意思。"五行"又有相克的关系：水克火，火克金，金克木，木克土，土克水。"克"有克服、战胜的意思。"五行"中的每一种物质，分别对应一种"德"，因此"五行"对应"五德"。每一种"德"代表一种特定的统治。黄帝时代是"土德"，夏朝是"木德"，商代为"金德"，周朝为"火德"。如今秦朝替代周朝，依照土、木、金、火、水"五德"循环更替的说法，就是秦朝代表的"水德"战胜了周朝的"火德"。所谓的五行相生、相克之说，有一些是有经验的依据，如木点燃，即生火；有火，用水浇灭，即水克火。古人认为五行相生相克是"客观规律"，因此，王朝按照五德循环替代，也就是不以人的意志为转移的了，即任何人都不能抗拒的。这样，秦王朝的兴起就具有了充分的合法性了。

那么，秦朝是不是"水德"呢？秦始皇的先祖秦文公曾外出打猎，捕获过黑龙。人们说，这就是"水德"的征兆。秦朝的先公五百年前就已经获得了"水德"的祥瑞，那么"水德"取代"火德"，秦朝取代周朝，便是必然的事情了。既然代表了"水德"，那么，秦朝就要按照"水德"的模式治理天下。"水德"的颜色是黑色，数字是六，于是，秦始皇便将"河水"

---

* *Yin and Yang*: the two opposing principles in nature, the former feminine and negative while the latter masculine and positive.

* *Wu Xing*: Wu means " five" and Xing means " element."

River (which is called the Yellow River today) into the Deshui River. He also gave the orders that October should be the first month of the year, and that the color black should be the color for imperial flags and garments. From what archeologists have excavated in Xianyang, the Qin capital, most of the buildings and portraits made during the Qin Dynasty were black. Evidence also suggests that six and its multiples were the emperor's favorite numbers. For example, the emperor's chariot was drawn by six horses, and the right size for the imperial crown was set at six *cun** long. By Qin Shihuang's order, 12 (a multiple of six) bronze statues were made from the collected weapons after his unification of China, each weighing 12 000 kilograms. In the ceremony where he offered sacrifices to the gods and his ancestors, he wore a crown with 12 strings of jade beads hanging from the top. Likewise, Qin Shihuang also divided his empire into 36 prefectures.

According to the *Yin-Yang* theory and the theory of the *Wu Xing*, water is of the nature of *Yin*, and it also stands for punishment and killing. Therefore, Qin Shihuang ruled his county with an iron fist, imposing harsh punishments on lawbreakers. The laws of the Qin Dynasty are too numerous to mention, but suffice it to say that the emperor established strict laws that covered nearly every aspect of life, all of which were rigorously enforced.

Emperor Ying Zheng possessed many qualities of a great and influential ruler. His importance as a historical figure not only derives from his unification of China, nor due to his ostentatious and extravagant lifestyle, nor even because he exhibited the stateliness and majesty of an emperor. Such superficial qualities can be found in many other historical rulers; what sets Qin Shihuang apart is that he possessed an unusual thirst for power which outshone that of any Chinese rulers before him. His relentless pursuit of power, as well as his determination to keep it for himself, shows him as an ideal model for a study on the impact that great power has on an individual.

Emperor Ying Zheng's profound intuition and brilliant imagination played an important role in his quest for power. Before the Qin Dynasty, there were only two types of supreme power. One was the power possessed by the emperors of the Zhou Dynasty when the dynasty was at the height of majesty and splendor. The other was the power held by some overlords during the Spring and Autumn Period, such as King Huan of Qi and King Wen of Jin. But neither of these types of power could satisfy Emperor Ying Zheng. For him, having supreme power meant that he exercised absolute control over everything within his view; in his mind, absolute power meant he could control everything. The Qin Empire was designed to begin with him, the first

改名为"德水","河水"就是现代的黄河。改每年的十月作为一年的第一个月，旗帜衣服以黑色最为尊贵。从秦都咸阳遗址的考古发掘来看，秦代的建筑和人物画一般为黑色。在所有的数字之中，崇尚"六"，因此六与六的倍数特别受到偏爱：皇帝的乘车，驾驭六匹马；皇帝头戴的皇冠，以六寸为规范；秦始皇销毁天下兵器，铸造六的倍数——十二尊铜像，每个铜人重二十四万斤；祭祀时皇帝头上戴的冠冕，悬垂十二条玉串；秦始皇最初把天下分为三十六个郡。

从阴阳五行家的观点来说，水属于阴，主管刑杀，所以秦始皇按照"水德"的要求，实行法治，并以刑罚为主。秦朝的法律条文很多，在各方面都有严格的规定，并且执法极为严厉。

秦王嬴政确实具有帝王的气质。这并不完全是说，秦王统一天下，号称"始皇帝"，自然具有了帝王的仪仗、排场、威严与风度。这些东西仅仅是帝王的外表，许多君主都可以做得到，甚至可能比秦王做得更像一位帝王。我们说秦王具有真正的帝王气质，是想说，秦王对于权力有一种远远超过一般君主的强烈渴望。这种渴望，包括追求权力、保持权威的各种才能，并不是所有帝王都充分具备的。对于权力的研究而言，秦始皇无疑是极好的范本。

对于权力他有一种深刻的直觉与超凡的想象。秦以前，最高权力的类型不外两种，一是如西周鼎盛时期的周天子，一是如春秋时期齐桓公、晋文公那样的霸主。可是这两种类型都不能满足秦王对于权力的欲求。对于秦王而言，权力意味着所有的一切都在他的掌握之中，都在他的视野之内，都在他的支配之下。他想象着在他拥有如此绝对权力的基础之上，秦帝国

---

* *cun*: a Chinese unit of length.

emperor, and then to be passed down to his descendants, the Second, the Third, and so on forever. Qin Shihuang saw power as a scepter that he could see and touch, and desired that his descendants should keep hold of it forever after him.

During the wars of the seven states, many believed that Ying Zheng, the Qin King, wished to achieve a position of overlord among the states. However, in actuality, he sought to eliminate all other independent powers and establish his own sovereign authority. It was not until he had nearly conquered all of the other states that they realized his true goals, and began to condemn him for his wild ambition.

The Qin Dynasty operated under an administrative system called the "Jun-Xian System," or the system of prefectures and counties. Aside from practical organizational matters, employing this system had much to do with Qin Shihuang's ardent pursuit of power.

After he had unified the states, Qin Shihuang faced a major dilemma: How was he to govern such a vast land? Most of his ministers and officials took their ideological foundation for government from past systems, but a stable system of governing a large country had not existed since the early Zhou Dynasty. At that time, the rulers based their government of the nation on their kinship with the lords of various states. The kings of Zhou divided the territory of the country among their relatives of the same clan in hopes that their family would retain firm control of their lands. In this way, the kings established strong ties with local governments. However, in later years, the Zhou kings gradually lost their connections to these local governments and ruled in name only, with the real power lying in the hands of powerful regional lords. Toward the end of the Zhou Dynasty, the lords did not even bother to acknowledge the king of Zhou symbolically, and they finally rebelled and declared themselves as kings. Hoping to consolidate the stability of the new Qin Empire, Wang Wan, the prime minister, advocated a traditional feudal system. Wang Wan suggested to the emperor, "We have just wiped out the six states, and the regions governed by the former states of Yan, Qi and Chu are all far away from our capital, Xianyang. Without new kings, we will be unable to govern these places; thus Your Majesty would be wise to send your princes there to be provincial kings."

Qin Shihuang then discussed Wang Wan's suggestion with his ministers and officials, and most of them agreed with the prime minister. But only Li Si, disagreed. Li Si counseled, "In the time of the Zhou Dynasty, King Wen and King Wu all granted territories to their kinsmen by blood. But after time, the

从他始皇帝开始，二世、三世至于万世，传之无穷。权力变成了一根看得见、摸得着、完全不会从帝王手中消失的权杖。

七国混战之时，一般人以为秦王只是想争取霸主的地位，他们不知道，秦王是要消灭其他一切自主的权力形式，建立自己至高无上的权威。后来人们看到了这一点，称秦国是狼子野心、虎狼心。

在行政体制上，秦王朝推行郡县制，这虽然有当时现实与历史方面的因素，但与秦始皇对权力的追求不无关系。

秦始皇统一天下后，如何治理如此广阔的疆域确实是一个大问题。当时的大臣中，大部分人的思维还局限在西周和春秋战国以来的政治框架内。周朝在国家政权的建设中，对地方的控制是通过血缘关系来维持的。周天子将自己的宗亲分封到各地做诸侯王，通过与诸侯王的血缘关系来维系地方与中央的关系。秦朝的丞相王绾就主张实行传统的分封制，以维护帝国的安定。王绾对秦始皇建议说："现在六国诸侯刚刚被消灭，燕国、齐国、楚国旧地，距离咸阳非常遥远，如果不在那些地方安排诸侯王，就没有办法管理，所以请将诸位王子派到那里去做王。"

秦始皇让大臣们讨论这一意见，群臣大都赞同王绾的建议，只有李斯提出了反对的意见。李斯说："周文王、周武王分封同姓子弟很多，但是时间一久，诸侯国之间的关系越来越疏远，

relationship between those feudal princes deteriorated into mutual hostility. They fought with one another for their own interests, and the Zhou kings could do nothing about it. Thus I declare that feudalism is not the answer to a stable government. Owing to Your Majesty's invincible might, we have finally unified the seven states. Many princes, ministers, and officers have made great contributions to this achievement, for which we should reward them—but with revenue instead of land. We should pay governors with revenue instead of merely granting them land to do with as they please. In this way, Your Majesty would have complete control over the entire nation, and it would also be less likely that the regional governors would seek for land or power. This is the fundamental principle of preserving social peace and order."

The system of prefectures and counties advocated by Li Si was nothing new for early in the Spring and Autumn Period, many states had such a system of counties. King Xiao of Qin had once divided his state into 41 counties, and this system was observed from that time on. Over the prefectures of unification, the Qin State made all the newly-conquered lands prefectures instead of granting them as vassal lands. That was why Wang Jian complained that as a meritorious general it was impossible for him to be raised to the peerage of a marquis.

Prefectures were administrative units directly under the central government. In every prefecture, there were such officials as prefecture chief, deputy chief, supervisor, and so on. Chiefs and deputy chiefs were in charge of administration and military affairs respectively, and supervisors managed the affairs of the prefecture government. The co-responsibility of these three officials was to preserve the law and order in the prefecture. Within each prefecture were many counties: Large counties were governed by county magistrates called "Xianling," and smaller counties were governed by heads of counties, or "Xianzhang," and both were responsible for the management of their counties. The leading officials of prefectures and counties were appointed by the central government. They received their salary (called "feng lu") from the government, and their posts could not be inherited by their descendants; in fact, they could be appointed to or removed from their posts at any time. This system was entirely different from the feudalist system. In feudalism, the titles and power of the lords of the land could be passed down to their descendants, allowing these lords to enjoy a degree of independence. For instance, they could appoint the officials in their respective lands. In this sense, the system of prefectures and counties more greatly concentrated the power and authority in the hands of the central government. Theoretically, the central power and

为了各自的利益，彼此相互攻击讨伐，周天子也无法禁止，这是很大的弊端。现在靠着陛下的神威，海内实现了统一，对于诸位王子和有功的大臣，用国家的赋税收入给予赏赐，这样便可以控制天下了。天下人没有非分（fèn）之想，是社会安宁的基本法则。分封诸侯并不合适。"

李斯主张全面实行郡县制。郡县制并不是新东西，在春秋时期已经出现。春秋时期不少诸侯国设有县制，秦孝公曾把秦国划为四十一个县。秦国在统一天下的过程中，对于新征服的地区，一律设郡，而不是分封诸侯。所以王翦抱怨："为大王将，有功终不得封侯。"

郡是中央直属的地方行政单位，每个郡设置郡守、郡尉、监御史等，分别负责行政、军事，监御史代表中央对郡实行监督，三官共同负责地方秩序。郡以下设立若干县，大县设令，小县设长，负责县一级地方管理。郡县主要的官员由中央任命，并领取一定的报酬即俸禄（fèng lù），他们的职位无法世袭，随时可以任免。这完全不同于诸侯国。诸侯国君主世袭，有程度不等的独立性，诸侯王有权任命诸侯国的官员。从这方面说，郡县制远比分封制更加集中了中央的权力，而中央的权力，理

authority were focused on the emperor. This system made it possible to effectively centralize state power, allowing the emperor to dominate government policies and also enabling him to maintain the country's unity with extended control over local governments.

Qin Shihuang agreed with Li Si's proposition. He said, "For many years our people have suffered through wars, which were caused by the existence of local lords. Now, owing to the blessing of my ancestors, we have returned peace and order to this country at last. However, if we retain a feudal system of government, then we will leave a latent danger of wars breaking out in the future; with numerous local lords, it will be difficult to maintain the peace we have established. Li Si's proposal is an excellent solution." Hereafter, the Qin Empire was divided into 36 prefectures, although later the number of prefectures increased to more than 40. In a sense, what the new empire did was merely extending to the whole empire the system already in place in the Qin State before unification. From that time on, all of the dynasties following the Qin have adopted this same form of government.

But the country-wide act of extending the system of prefectures and counties was fiercely contested by many scholars who firmly believed in Confucianism and revered the system of the West Zhou. This led to a debate on the system of prefectures and counties in 213 B.C.

In that year, Qin Shihuang held a feast for his ministers and officials in his palace at Xianyang, where 70 court scholars gave toasts to the emperor. One of them, a man name Zhou Qingchen, gave a speech in praise of Qin Shihuang. In this speech, he said, "Not long ago, the land of the Qin State only covered 1 000 square *li*. But now, thanks to Your Majesty's brilliance, we have brought peace and order back to the whole land. The barbarians have been driven out, and all the land which the sun and the moon shine over has become Your Majesty's domain. Prefectures and counties have been established in the areas ruled by former states. Now all the people live and work in peace and contentment and no longer suffer from the turmoil of war. Such a splendid achievement will be held in memory for ages to come. Since ancient times, no other kings or emperors have ever accomplished such a remarkable feat." Qin Shihuang was very pleased with this speech, but one court scholar named Chun Yuyue disagreed with Zhou Qingchen on the establishment of prefectures and counties. He said, "According to my knowledge, the only reason why the Yin and Zhou dynasties could last for more than a thousand years is that they gave lands to princes, or to generals or ministers who had rendered outstanding service to the state. These lords of vassal states supported

论上讲，是集中在皇帝的手中。郡县制从制度上有效地把权力集中在中央，有利于维护皇帝的主宰（zǎi）地位，有利于维护国家的统一和地方的治理。

秦始皇十分赞同李斯的意见，他说："天下遭受战争之苦已经很久了，根本原因就在于有诸侯存在。现在靠着祖先的神灵保佑，天下终于得到安定，如果再分封诸侯王，无疑将埋下战争的隐患。分封大大小小的诸侯，要想使天下安定，岂不困难！李斯的建议是正确的。"于是，秦朝决定把天下分为三十六个郡，后来又扩展到四十多个郡。从某种意义上讲，此时所推行的郡县制，只是将秦国原有的地方行政体制推广到整个中国。郡县制度后来成为历代王朝中央政权控制地方行政的基本形式。

在全国范围内推行郡县制的做法，不断地遭到许多信奉儒家经典、崇尚西周制度的学者的强烈质疑。这导致了秦始皇三十四年（公元前213年）的一场有关郡县制度的辩论。

秦始皇在咸阳宫中大宴群臣，七十个博士官为皇帝祝酒。一位叫周青臣的官员奉上了一段歌功颂德的祝酒辞："以往秦国的地盘不过方圆千里，今日靠陛下的神明，平定了海内，驱逐了蛮夷，日月所照的地方，全都成了陛下的国土。在诸侯统治的旧地设立郡县，人人安乐，不再有战争的祸患，这样的功业可以传之万世。自上古时代，没有一个帝王能赶得上陛下的威德。"秦始皇听了非常高兴。博士淳于越反对周青臣的"设立郡县"观点，进言道："我听说殷周的天下能维持一千多年，正是因为分封诸位王子和功臣，诸侯国相互支持。如今陛下拥

one another to maintain national stability. But now Your Majesty possesses the whole of this land. If we enact the system of prefectures and counties, then the princes will have no land, and will be forced to live as ordinary citizens. If disasters or rebellions occurred, then how could these princes support one another? We must reconsider and think this through; to my knowledge, I have never heard of a ruler achieving lasting success in his policies while turning his back on tradition."

In his speech, Chun Yuyue had spoken with sharp language, but Qin Shihuang did not respond with anger, nor with a retort of his own. Instead, he placed Chun's ideas before his ministers and officials, and asked them for their opinions on the matter.

Once again, it was Li Si who prevailed over the dissenting views. He said, "In the past, the policies of the Five Emperors were different from each other. People in the dynasties of Xia, Shang and Zhou did not follow the same policies, yet with these different policies they all achieved stability and prosperity. It was not that they changed policies on purpose, but that they changed their policies according to their individual circumstances. His Majesty's success in establishing this great empire seems to be beyond the comprehension of some in this room—and if we cannot fully appreciate the miracle of this empire, then can we truly understand the policies of the Xia, Shang and Zhou dynasties? Their policies are distant, and obscured by the tides of time, and as such we should establish a new system based on our current situation rather than relying on the ideas of an indistinct past."

Li Si criticized Chun Yuyue for his advocacy of returning to former policies, and continued to advocate the creation of a highly centralized imperial government. He said, "In the past, during the wars between lords of various states, the lords would employ travelers to spread rumors for them, thus spreading ideas across the land. Now, however, our country is unified. What husbandmen should do now is to promote the handicraft industry and agriculture. As for the scholars, they should focus on learning the new decrees and statutes. Yet some scholars here do not comprehend our current situation, and blindly follow past traditions. Their criticism of our new policies will leave the people confused... If we let these scholars concoct their own theories to criticize our policies, then these ideas will undermine the authority of the state and public opinions will turn against us. As such, it is our duty to ban all books that propose theories intending to undermine the state's authority. In the case of history books, we should have our historians keep the records of the Qin State and have all unorthodox historical records burned. Only court

有天下，推行郡县，诸位王子没有封地，和普通人一样，一旦有什么祸乱，诸位王子又该如何相救？做事不遵循传统而能够长久的，我没有听说过。"

淳于越的言语非常尖锐，作为一国之君的秦始皇并没有怒责淳于越，也没有立即裁断是非，而是把这个问题交给群臣来讨论。

这一次又是李斯力排众议，他说："远古时代五帝的政策并不完全相同，夏、商、周三代的制度不相沿袭，但各自都实现了国家的安定昌盛，并不是故意采取不一样的制度，而是随着时代、形势的变化而变化。如今陛下创立大业，建树万世的功德，这本来就不是愚笨的书生所能理解的。更何况所谓的三代制度，遥远渺茫，怎么能够效法？"

李斯严厉批判博士淳于越追随上古制度的观点，竭力推行严格管制、整体一元的社会秩序。他说："过去诸侯相互征战的时候，君主都以优厚的待遇请来各地的说客、游士为自己服务。这些游士传播着各种各样的思想。如今天下大定，有着统一的法令，百姓就是要积极促进手工业、农业的发展，士人就是要学习法令法规。可是现在的读书人不了解现实，却抱着旧的传统，谴责现行的政策，扰乱百姓的思想。……如果让这些私学存在，各以自行的一套学说来批评谴责当今的政策，君主的权威就要下降，而私学舆论就会形成对抗的势力。因此，必须禁止这些学说，只在史官那里保留秦国历史记载，其他国史

scholars should be allowed to study the books such as the *Book of Poems* and the *Book of Documents*, and others should be forbidden from keeping these books, or the writings of Confucius and other ancient classics. Those who own these books should send them to the local government to be burned. Anyone who dares to speak of ideas from the *Book of Poems* and the *Book of Documents* should be beheaded, and if anyone dares to criticize our new policies by citing examples from history, he and his entire family should be exterminated. Books on medicine, divination and agriculture, however, should be excluded from the books to be burned, and any who wish to learn about the decrees of the state should be able to receive that information freely from the state officials."

Later, Li Si's proposal served as the theoretical basis for the infamous book-burning of the Qin Dynasty, i.e., the burning of the *Book of Poems* and the *Book of Documents* as well as the texts of the hundred schools. Book-burning was an extreme attempt to silence criticism of the new imperial system. Though Qin had unified the country, noblemen from the former six states still remained, and some of them wished to restore what they had lost. There was also a general feeling of insecurity in the new empire, with a high probability that the people might incite a rebellion against the emperor. In the face of instability and political turmoil, Qin Shihuang had no choice but to take every precaution to suppress resistance. He adopted Li Si's idea and ordered the burning of many texts, as well as taking harsh measures to guard against dissent. From that time onward, none dared to criticize the system of prefectures and counties in public.

When King Xiao of Qin was in power, he put Shang Yang, a Legalist, in a high position of his state, thus enabling Shang Yang to enact a series of political reforms. For this reason, Legalism deeply influenced the policies and law codes of the Qin State. Qin Shihuang inherited this system of policies, and sought to uphold the traditions of Legalism in all of his imperial decrees, appointing officials who would strictly enforce the law to his highest posts of authority.

Li Si and others were commissioned to write the new state's constitution, *The Law of the Qin Dynasty*. Most of the content in *The Law of the Qin Dynasty* came from *The Book of Law* by Li Kui, a man in the Wei State during the Warring States Period. Shang Yang brought this book to the Qin State before he began his Legalist reforms. Over time, each successive Qin King modified the content of the book, until the final, more detailed, law of the Qin State emerged.

皆烧毁。只有博士官（官方学者）可以研究《诗》、《书》，其他人一律不得收藏《诗》、《书》、诸子百家之书，均送交当地官府烧毁。有敢谈论《诗》、《书》的人斩首。以古代批评现在的灭其宗族。医药卜筮（bǔ shì）种树之书，不在销毁之列。有人想要学习法令，以官吏为老师。"

这是秦代后来"焚书"事件，即焚烧《诗》、《书》以及诸子百家之书的理论基础。它试图以一种极端的手段解决当时遭遇到的社会治理的压力。秦国统一天下，但是六国残余力量仍然存在，贵族仍然向往回到过去的富贵生活，人心浮动，发动叛乱的可能性并没有完全消除。这样的政治形势，迫使秦始皇处处考虑增强自己的权威，压制一切可能的反抗。秦始皇采纳了李斯的建议，随后又采取"焚书"的手段，打击那些持不同意见的人。从此以后，再也没有人敢于公开批评郡县制度。

自秦孝公任用商鞅变法以来，秦国的政治和法律深受法家思想的影响。秦始皇继承了秦国法治的传统，强调以严格的法律治理国家，任用执法严格的官吏，在各个领域一丝不苟地按照法律办事。

李斯等人主持制定了《秦律》。《秦律》的基本内容来源于战国时期魏国李悝（kuī）的《法经》。商鞅变法时，把它带到秦国，后来的几代君王对《法经》逐步完善，形成了比较详细的秦朝法律。

The provisions of *The Law of the Qin Dynasty* covered nearly all aspects of life, and there were numerous strict regulations that the people had to live by. The punishment for breaking these laws was severe; lawbreakers would be subject to harsh penalties for even small offenses, and the methods of punishment were innumerable. This harsh system was characteristic of Qin Shihuang's policy of rule by law.

In 1975, in a place called Shui Hu (sleeping tiger) in the county of Yunmeng in Hubei Province, archeologists unearthed bamboo slips from a tomb of the Qin Dynasty on which many items of Qin law were carved. They include statutes involving civil, administrative, economical and military affairs, as well as laws for penal offenses and lawsuits. They touched upon everything from agriculture—such as management of farmland, water conservation, protection of mountain forests, cattle raising and horse raising— to civic affairs, such as construction projects, market business, grain preservation, and the appointment and dismissal of officials. The laws are very specific in their wording. For instance, *The Law of Preserving Grain in Depots* stipulated in great detail the methods of selecting, preserving, and sowing seeds, and the numbers and kinds of crops farmers should grow. *The Law of Farmland* forbad people from stripping the land and hunting young animals. It is evident from these laws that people of the Qin Dynasty respected nature and emphasized the preservation of natural resources.

In *The Law of the Qin Dynasty,* we find a system of law in which there are many specific provisions for the management of industry and commerce. *The Law of Accounting and Statistics* stipulated in great detail the permitted error in measurements. *The Law of Craft* required standardization of products and banned any alteration of the standard specifications. In *The Law of Miscellaneous Affairs,* one clause stipulates that officials should not profit from the abuse of power, the punishment of which is banishment. The ruling class of this newly established dynasty also desired that their laws should be widely read and understood. Thus they compiled *Answers for Questions on the Law,* in which they provided very detailed explanations of the law in the form of questions and answers, increasing the law's accessibility to the common people. Qin law also specified the legal process of hearing cases, the proper formatting of legal documents, and the code of professional ethics for government officials. The legal system of the Qin Dynasty was the most complete and precise in Chinese history, a landmark in the development of Chinese law.

Penalties for breaking Qin laws were characterized by their ruthlessness

秦朝的法律条文相当完备，在各方面规定均很严格，处罚严厉。轻罪重罚，繁密苛刻，是秦始皇以法治国的特点。

1975年在湖北省云梦县睡虎地秦墓出土了大量记载秦代法律文书的竹简《秦律十八种》。这批竹简包括有民法、行政法、经济法、军法、刑法、诉讼法等十多个法律门类。涉及的内容相当广泛，包括农田水利的管理、山林的保护、牛马的饲养、工程兴建、市场买卖、粮库保管、官员任免等。有关的法律规定十分详细、具体、明确。如《仓律》中对种子的选择、保管、使用和各类农作物播种数量进行了规定。《田律》中有禁止滥伐山林，禁止捕猎幼兽的规定。这说明秦王朝非常重视保护自然资源和人与自然之间的关系。

《秦律》中对工商业的管理有严格而系统的规定，内容相当丰富。《效律》中对度量衡的误差限度有明确说明；《工律》规定同一产品必须规格一样，严禁改变产品制造标准。《秦律杂抄》中有一条法律规定：严禁官吏利用职权进行盈利活动，否则处以流放的重刑。秦朝很重视法律的普及，在《法律答问》中采用问答形式对各种法律条文、术语和律文的意图进行了详细的解释，十分有利于一般民众对法律的了解。秦时的法律还指定了审理案件的程序、法律文书的格式，同时对政府官员的职业道德和行为准则也作出了规范。秦朝法律体系的完备和精密程度可以说是前无古人，堪称中国古代法律史上的里程碑。

刑罚的严酷是秦王朝法制的突出特点。在秦朝的法律中，

and cruelty. For example, there are more than 20 ways that the death penalty could be carried out, including cutting a man's belly open, pulling out his tendons, and burying him alive. If the man to be executed was caught swearing, his tongue would be cut off first before he was put to death. For those who were found guilty of treason against the state, not only would they be executed, but their family members were also sentenced to death, as if they had committed the same crime. The more serious the punishment to the offender, the higher the chance that family members would suffer the same fate. To the modern mind, these punishments might seem too appalling to be true, but they were part of Qin Shihuang's severe legal system.

During the Qin Dynasty's rule, even small offenses earned harsh punishments. The law stipulated that if five men committed theft together, and the worth of the things they stole was above one copper coin, their toes would be cut off; if someone stole mulberry leaves whose worth was less than one copper coin, he would be sentenced to 30 days' servitude. There were, too, some kinds of punishment meant to humiliate or abase, such as flogging and shaving their beard or hair. The ancient Chinese viewed having beard or hair shaved as a source of great humiliation to a man and his entire family, as they believed that hair and beard were gifts given by a man's parents, and that it would be unfilial to shave them. Aside from principal penalties, there were also many accessory penalties in Qin law, which only served to increase the severity and cruelty of punishment. Qin Shihuang made every effort to stretch the law's influence over the entire country, hoping to regulate his newly-established regime by forcing all to comply with his decrees. However, the harshness of his penalties and the extreme measures that the emperor took to ensure obedience were too much for the people to bear. Intense discontentment with his policies and resistance among the people grew, setting the stage for the Qin Dynasty's eventual collapse.

规定有一系列残酷的刑罚，仅死刑便有二十多种，现代看起来相当残酷，如剖腹、抽筋、活埋等。如果犯人谩（màn）骂，须先割下犯人的舌头，然后再受刑。秦朝还实行连坐，就是对危害国家统治的犯人，其亲属也会连带受到处罚，罪犯的刑罚越重，连坐的范围越广。

　　秦朝法律实行轻罪重罚的原则。五人共同盗窃一钱以上财物就要斩断脚趾；偷人桑叶价值不到一钱，要罚劳役三十天。秦律中还有一种教刑，即用鞭笞、羞辱等方式惩戒罪犯，例如剃光罪犯的胡须、毛发。中国古代社会的观念认为，人的身体头发都是父母给的，不能够毁伤，否则就是不孝，因此，犯罪被剔去毛发是个人与家族的耻辱。秦朝的各种附加刑种类也比较多，使酷刑变得更加严厉。秦始皇力图设置一个严密的法网，使社会生活的各个层面都有法可依，从而巩固新生的政权。然而由于秦朝刑罚过于繁密和严酷，人民时时处在紧张压迫的环境之中，激起了人民强烈的不满与反抗，这加速了秦王朝的覆灭。

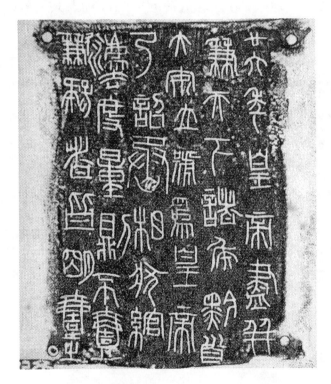

秦代的文字

Chinese characters in the Qin Dynasty

八　统一度量衡与文字

Chapter Ⅷ　Standardization of Metrology and Characters

The people of the Qin State had a fondness for precision, and Shang Yang also had a keen interest in precise calculations in measurement. Qin craftsmen also held to universal standards of measurement and could produce items with a high degree of precision. For example, the unearthed terracotta warriors and horses were created with such precise standards that many of their parts can be replaced by any of the same part of another. Not only did the Qin people value the idea of standardization, but they had also taken measures by this time to ensure that it was followed. Thus, after the Qin Emperor unified China, he established imperial standards of weights and measures on which commerce and states taxes heavily relied.

The term "metrology" refers to the measurement of the length, size (cubage) and weight of an object. If these measurements lack an established standard, then it is extremely troublesome in trade and industry to convert between different systems. Before the unified Qin Empire, due to wars and political instability, the currency and the standards of weight and measurement varied enormously from one state to another. In the Qin State, one *chi** was about 23 cm, while in some other places it was a little longer than 23 cm. In the Qi State people used *sheng* as the unit of dry measure for grain (one *sheng* was about 164 milliliters) while in the Qin State they used *dou*, which was about 200 milliliters. The standard of measurement for weight in all those states was almost the same (one *jin* was equal to 16 *liang*), but the actual weight was different. For instance, in the Chu State, one *jin* was about 251 grams, while in Qin it was about 256 grams. The differences in metrology caused great inconvenience in trade and in levying taxes.

After unification, the barriers between the former states had been removed. To promote economic exchange across the new empire and encourage communication, Qin Shihuang ordered standards set for metrology and currency. In this way, the standards of weight and measurement established during Shang Yang's reforms were extended to the entire country in the year that the emperor came to power (221 B.C.).

To ensure that standardization would spread throughout the country, Qin Shihuang ordered the construction of a standard apparatus of weights and measures, and then had it copied and distributed throughout the land. The full text of the imperial decree for standardization was engraved on each apparatus. The "Tongquan (copper scale)" made in the Qin Dynasty is similar to the one that the Chinese use in modern times. The inscription on this copper scale reads: "Twenty-six years after he came to the throne, Qin Shihuang eliminated the other states and completed his great undertaking of unification. From that

秦人喜爱精确。商鞅对计量的精确有浓厚的兴趣，秦国的工匠制作的部件规格统一，精度很高。出土的秦朝兵马俑，许多相同的部件都可以任意替换，说明秦人已经有标准化的意识与措施。对于一个地区的贸易、税收所依赖的度量衡，秦人更是强调统一与标准。

度、量、衡分别指物体的长度、体积（容积）和重量的单位以及相关的称量。它们如果不统一，在实际的操作过程中，换算十分麻烦。统一以前，由于长期的对抗与纷争，各诸侯国之间的货币与度量衡的标准存在很大的差异。秦国的1尺大约相当于23厘米，而有些地方的1尺则稍长一些；齐国的"量"以升为单位，1升约合164毫升，秦国以"斗（dǒu）"为单位，1斗合200毫升；各国的"衡"大体上都是1斤约等于16两，但实际重量并不一样，如楚国1斤约合251克，秦国则相当于256克。度量衡之间的差异给地区之间的贸易活动带来不便，也不利于征收赋税。

秦始皇统一全国后，原先诸侯国之间的壁垒（bì lěi）关卡消除了。为了有效地促进全国各地的经济交流和人民往来，秦始皇统一中国的当年（公元前221年），颁布了统一的度量衡与货币的法令，即将商鞅变法时确立的度量衡标准推行到全国范围。

为了保证顺利推广，秦始皇命令制作统一标准的度量衡器，颁发到全国各地，并在上面刻上皇帝的诏书全文。我们现在还能看到秦朝统一制作的"铜权"。铜权类似于今天的砝码，铜权上有铭文，意思说："二十六年，秦始皇吞灭诸侯，完成了

---

* *chi*: a Chinese unit of length, 3 *chi*=1 meter.

time on, the people all lived in peace and security. The emperor took upon himself the new title of 'Huang Di.' He then ordered Wang Wan, his prime minister, to affix standards for length, volume and weight, and by his command, all confusing decrees were clearly defined and standardized."

Qin Shihuang also took measures to ensure that the new standards of metrology were followed. By his order, the apparatus of weights and measurements should be checked at least once a year, and those who were found using any nonstandard apparatus would incur fines.

In the meantime, Qin Shihuang also issued imperial decrees to standardize currency. During the Warring States Period, clothing currency circulated in the states of Han and Wei, while in the states of Qi, Yan and Zhao, people used knife-shaped copper money, and in the state of Chu, the people used tiny seashell-like coins. In the Qin State, people used round coins with a square hole in the middle. After the unification, Qin Shihuang had all other currency invalidated, and by his order, the money of the former Qin State was used all over China, with gold as the hard currency and with pearls, jades, tortoise's shells and silver reduced to collectors' items instead of money.

The government of the Qin Dynasty also controlled the right to make currency, and people without permission were forbidden from making coins. There are records in the bamboo slips unearthed in Yunmeng about cases of confiscating the coins made without permission. Because of its convenience, the form of the money of the Qin Dynasty continued to be used for more than 2 000 years.

The unification of weights, measures, and currency was extremely vital for the newly-established dynasty to consolidate its political order and promote economic development.

One ancient Chinese scholar pointed out, "Food is the people's first necessity." Agriculture formed the economic backbone of the largely agrarian Qin Empire.

When the new dynasty was founded, some people concealed the amount their fields from the government so that they could evade taxes. In order to stop this, 31 years after he came to power (216 B.C.), Qin Shihuang ordered that farmland all over the country be registered. Many farmers had been allotted land, and this had greatly promoted their enthusiasm for production. According to the laws of the time, farmers could borrow iron farm tools from the local governments, and when their tools fell into disrepair, the farmers could replace them by informing government officials. In addition, in order to improve agricultural production, Qin Shihuang built the Lingqu Canal, had the

统一大业，人民从此有了安定的生活环境。于是立尊号为'皇帝'，令丞相王绾等负责统一度量衡的标准。对于那些使人疑惑的法令，都应当使其明确、统一。"

秦始皇还以法律形式确保度量衡的标准，规定每年至少检校（jiào）一次，对不准确的度量衡器，给予经济处罚。

秦始皇在统一度量衡的同时，也颁布了统一货币的诏令。六国时，韩、魏流通布币，齐、燕、赵流通刀币，楚国流通形状像海贝的蚁鼻钱，秦国流通圆形的半两钱。统一后，秦始皇下令废除原各诸侯国发行的货币，以原来秦国的方孔圆形钱币为通用货币。黄金作为上等货币使用。珠玉、龟贝、银锡之类作为器饰收藏，不再作为货币使用。

秦朝还统一货币的铸造，把铸造权收归中央，禁止私人铸造钱币，云梦出土的秦简中就记载着没收私人铸币的案例。秦朝的方孔圆形钱币，由于使用方便，在中国一直沿用了两千多年。

度量衡与货币的统一，对于维护秦王朝的政治秩序、促进经济发展，有着重大的意义。

"民以食为天"，对于一个以自然经济为主的国家而言，农业是国家的经济命脉。

秦始皇三十一年（公元前216年），秦始皇下令在全国范围内对民田进行登记，防止私人隐匿（nì）田亩，影响国家的赋税收入。农民有了自己的土地，劳动积极性大大提高了。秦朝的法律规定，农民可以向政府借铁农具，如果农具破损，官员把它记录下来就可以了，农民不必赔偿。秦始皇还主持了灵渠

country's irrigation works extended, and provided ample water for the vast tracts of land in the Xing' an area (the present city of Guiling in Guangxi Province). Due to irrigation, the Qin Dynasty built up ample stores of grain in its capital. According to historical records, when the army led by Liu Bang* captured Xianyang, the people of the city offered Liu Bang and his army large quantity of cattle, sheep, wine and grain.

Though it was primarily an agrarian state, the Qin Dynasty enacted policies that also expanded its industries and commerce. For this reason, industries such as ore smelting underwent considerable development. According to historical records, there was a widow woman in Sichuan named Qing, whose family had mined cinnabar for several generations. The woman created a thriving business and earned a large amount of property for her family. Qin Shihuang appreciated the woman so much that after the woman died he had a monumental platform built in her honor, which was named "Nü Huai Qing Tai." Even though Qing was merely an ordinary woman living in a remote corner of the empire, the honor that the emperor bestowed upon her made her famous across the land for her business sense. Another man named Zhuo, also from the Sichuan area, achieved commercial success in a similar way. Zhuo was a native of the Zhao State before the unification. After his native state was annexed by the Qin State, by Qin Shihuang's order he and his entire family moved to Sichuan, where they began a business of smelting iron ore. He sold the iron they made to various cities across the land, and with the money his family earned, they built themselves splendid mansions and bought a vast forest for hunting.

By the time of the Qin Dynasty, copper smelting workshops were already prevalent among the Qin cities. At the historic site of Xianyang, archaeologists have discovered a copper smelting workshop which is 150 meters long and 60 meters wide—a total area of 9 000 square meters. In front of the Epang Palace*, stood 12 bronze statues, each weighing 12 000 kilograms. Many fittings of bronze chariots were also unearthed from the mausoleum of Qin Shihuang; each fitting weighs 1 000 kilograms, and is composed of more than 7 000 parts. People marvel even today at the great technical skill of Qin-era bronze casting.

There were also businessmen among the people of Qin who worked in the livestock industry and became fabulously wealthy. For example, a businessman named Luo lived in Gansu, an area in western China. Luo bartered for silk from the east with his animals. Then he sold the silk to the chieftains of the surrounding tribesmen, who would pay him in animals ten

的修建，扩大了水利事业，灌溉了兴安地区（今广西桂林）的大片农田。秦朝的粮仓积蓄（xù）很多，在刘邦攻入首都咸阳的时候，秦人献给刘邦的军队许多牛羊及酒食。

尽管秦朝以农为主，但并不限制工商业，而是把它引入正常的法制轨道，因而秦朝的工商业也取得了较大的发展，尤其是冶矿业。四川地区有一位寡妇，名叫清，她家历代经营朱砂矿，很有成就，家财不可计算。秦始皇赞赏她，专门为她修筑了一座女怀清台。后人感叹道："清是一名偏僻穷乡的寡妇，竟然得到皇帝的礼遇，名扬天下，不正是因为拥有很多的财富吗？"在四川地区还有一位姓卓的人，以冶铁致富。他原来是赵国人，秦灭赵以后，秦始皇将其家迁到了四川。卓家从事冶铁业，并把铁具卖到全国各地，还给自己修了很多游玩和射猎的场地。

秦朝的冶铜作坊已经具有相当大的规模。在秦都咸阳旧址，考古学家发现了一处冶铜作坊，南北150米，东西60米，面积达9 000平方米，可见其规模之大。秦王的宫殿阿房宫前站立12个铜人，每个铜人重达24万斤。秦始皇陵墓中出土的铜车马，重达2 000多斤，由7 000多个部件组成，即使现代人也叹为观止。

秦朝还有一些以经营畜牧业而富甲一方的商人。如在中国西部甘肃有个叫倮（luǒ）的人，他经营畜牧业，用牲畜（chù）换取东部的丝绸，再把丝绸贩卖给一些少数民族的首

---

*   Liu Bang: (256~195 B.C.) the first emperor of the Han Dynasty, also known as Emperor Gaozu of Han.
*   Epang Palace: built on a large scale and with a majestic style, was the imperial palace of the first and second emperors of the Qin Dynasty (221~206B.C.). During wars at the end of the Qin Dynasty, Xiang Yu captured Xianyang City and burned down the splendid Epang Palace.

times the number that he had paid the easterners for the silk. Soon the number of Luo's animals was not counted by herds or flocks, but by valleys. Qin Shihuang offered Luo, too, a reward and allowed him to participate in state affairs with the ministers.

Language is the symbol of a nation's culture, and also the medium for transferring culture. Since ancient times, the Chinese nation has retained a continuous cultural heritage, despite government fragmentations and foreign invasions. Whenever it seemed that their culture would be destroyed, the Chinese people gained a greater sense of cohesion to survive the crisis. One critical reason that the Chinese sense of national identity persists so strongly even today is that China has a uniform written language.

The Chinese system of written characters has a long history. It can be traced far back into Yin and Shang dynasties, in which a relatively systemized written language is preserved in oracle bone inscriptions. In the Zhou Dynasty, people used the system of "Dazhuan" as their way of writing characters. But this complicated system made it difficult for people to write, not to mention that the forms of characters varied from place to place. During the Spring and Autumn Period, due to the long-time independent regimes of the various states as well as differences in geography, climate, and people in these states, usage of characters was also varied. One character had different forms in different states, and some even had several variations within the same state. Take the word "horse" for instance: In the Qi State, there were two ways to write this word, while in the states of Han, Zhao and Wei, the same word was written in two other different ways. And in the states of Chu and Yan, it was written in another two totally different ways, meaning that the word "horse" could be written at least 10 different ways. The same word with numerous variant forms kept people from communicating with each other effectively across regions.

For this new dynasty, having so many variants of the written language made it impossible for an effective administration which depended on written documents. For instance, the imperial decrees, as well as the country-wide registration of households and land distribution, were transcribed in the form of writs. Without these writs, it would be impossible to effectively implement an administrative system.

After the establishment of the empire, the emperor ordered Li Si to begin the work of standardizing Chinese characters by removing forms of words different from Qin's. Li Si made "Xiaozhuan" from the former state of Qin the standard writing system for the entire empire. He also, however, incorporated some qualities of "Dazhuan" into the newly standardized script. In this way, he

领，这些首领就会给他十倍的牲畜。倮的牲畜多到要用山谷来计算。秦始皇给予他奖赏，允许他与朝中大臣一样，参与国家事务。

文字是一个民族文明的标志，也是民族文明传承的载体。中华民族的历史文化从遥远的古代一直延续到今天，从未断裂，在遭遇分裂和外敌入侵面前，中华民族都能够形成相当大的凝聚力和认同感，这在一定程度上得益于中国有统一的书写文字。

中国的汉字源远流长。殷商时期已经有较为系统的甲骨文。周朝有"大篆（zhuàn）"体的文字，大篆字体笔画复杂，书写比较困难，字形也不十分统一。到春秋战国时期，由于诸侯国的长期割据，加上各地的地理、气候、民族等因素的差异，文字在使用的过程中出现了不同的变异。各国之间乃至一国之内，文字字形上的差异很大。如"马"字的写法就有很多。在齐国的文字中，"马"字有两种写法；在韩、赵、魏三国，"马"字是另外的两种写法；楚、燕两国，又完全是两种不同的写法。这样，一个"马"字便有十种不同的写法。相同的字却有许多不同的书写字形，这在很大程度上阻碍了人们思想和文化的交流。

对于秦王朝而言，混乱的文字书写，很不利于行政的运行。行政的运行依赖大量的文书，如皇帝发布的诏令、全国各地的户籍登记、土地分配的登记等，都会以书写的形式形成文书。如果没有这些文书，就不可能建立起复杂庞大的行政管理体制。因此，书写在根本上与权力有关。

秦朝立国后，秦始皇命令李斯主持文字的统一工作，废除与秦文字不同的其他文字。李斯在原秦国篆体文字的基础上，吸取大篆的长处，创造了笔画简略、字体齐整的"小篆"字体。

created the small seal script characters (known as "Xiaozhuan") with simpler strokes and neater forms. In order to give people a sample of the new standard writing system, Li Si, Zhao Gao and Hu Wujing each wrote an article in the new style: "On Cang Xie*" (by Li Si), "On Yuanli" (by Zhao Gao), and "On Erudition" (by Hu Wujing). These articles were all used as primary materials in teaching children to read. When Qin Shihuang made his inspection tours throughout the country, each place would record his trip by carving it on stones or rocks in "Xiaozhuan," and all official documents were also similarly written in "Xiaozhuan."

At the same time, many people also used another writing style, called "Lishu." Lishu was allegedly invented by a man called Cheng Miao, a former inferior official in a county government who was thrown into prison for committing a crime for more than 10 years. While in jail, he devoted himself to working on modifying the written characters, and after 10 years in prison, he created the Lishu characters, which were easier to write than the Xiaozhuan ones. With this style of writing, the strokes of characters were simpler and the characters looked somewhat square but beautiful. He wrote an article of more than 3 000 characters in this style, and had it submitted to Qin Shihuang. The emperor was pleased with this style of writing, and soon Lishu (also known as official script) became popular among the common people. Archeologists working at sites in Yunmeng have discovered two soldiers' letters to their families, both written in Lishu. As rule by law was a fundamental principle of the Qin Dynasty, officials prepared a large number of hand-written documents to issue decrees daily. Due to the increasing complexity of administration in the Qin government, the officials needed a simpler writing system than the complicated Xiaozhuan to keep up with the high number of writings issued. In order to save time and foster efficiency, the imperial government allowed officials to write less important documents in Lishu, though they were still required to write important documents, such as imperial decrees, in Xiaozhuan. The Lishu system laid the foundation for Kaishu, the standard script (or regular script) of handwriting which came into being sometime later, and represented a reasonable trend of development in the Chinese characters. Lishu is an important milestone in the history of Chinese characters.

Simplifying and standardizing the written language for the Qin Empire is out of the necessity of unification, which actually has exerted great and profound influence on Chinese Culture. As China is a vast country where its people speak hundreds of different dialects according to where they live, the standardization of Chinese characters provided greater opportunity for inter-

为了在书写时有统一的规范，秦始皇令李斯作《仓颉（xié）篇》，赵高作《爰（yuán）历篇》，胡毋敬作《博学篇》，作为学童的识字课本。秦始皇巡行全国各地时，刻在石头上的文字都是用小篆书写，当时的官方正式文书也都是用小篆书写。

当时民间还通行隶书。传说，有个叫程邈（chéng miǎo）的县吏，因犯罪被关在狱中十多年。他在狱中专心致志地研究汉字的书写，花了十年的功夫，创造了一种更加容易书写的字体。这种字体笔画简单，字体方形美观，书写起来比小篆方便得多。他用这种字体写了一篇三千多字的文章，秦始皇见到后很欣赏。隶书成为民间流行的书写字体。在云梦秦墓中出土的两封战士的家信，都是用隶书书写。秦朝重视法治，狱案繁多，官吏需要书写大量的公文。为了节省时间，提高效率，秦朝允许隶书作为官府一般性文件的书写字体，但重要的诏书还是用小篆书写。隶书奠定了楷（kǎi）书的基础，代表着汉字字形的合理发展方向，是中国文字发展史上的一个里程碑。

秦朝简化、规范汉字的出发点本是帝国统一的需要，但客观上对中国文化的发展产生了极其重大而深远的影响。中国疆域辽阔，各地的方言千差万别，文字的统一，不仅给跨地区之

---

* Cang Jie: the inventor of Chinese characters in legend.

regional communication, as well as for further cultural and economic development. It was essential in the rapid development of the Chinese cultural community as well as in shaping the people's unique Chinese identity. Qin Shihuang played an indispensable role in developing the Chinese language, allowing it to further influence the development of Chinese culture.

间的经济文化交流提供了便利，而且对中华文化共同体的迅速发展和中华民族统一心理的塑造也具有巨大的推动意义。汉语和汉字历经数千年的发展，成为世界上最具表现力的语系之一。在这一发展过程中，秦始皇的作用确实不可忽视。

兵马俑
Terracotta warriors and horses

九　开拓边疆

Chapter Ⅸ　Expanding the Frontier

One significant characteristic of the newly-established Qin Empire was its vast territory. Even after unifying the six states, Qin Shihuang was still not content with the land he had. Five or six years later, once the country had somewhat recovered from the last war, he began another bold endeavor to expand the borders of his empire.

To the north of the Qin Empire lived a nomadic pastoral people called the Huns. The Huns were nomadic tribes, who for many years lived around the northern frontier areas of China. Proficient in riding horses and shooting arrows, the men of the Huns were unusually bold and possessed great physical strength. Whenever Qin's defenses slackened, they would not hesitate to raid areas on the frontier, capturing peasants and plundering the cities, and as such they were seen as a great threat to the Qin Empire. During the Warring States Period, the states of Qin, Yan and Zhao all faced the threat of the the Huns, and these states were particularly on guard against the Hun's invasion. When Queen Mother Xuan ruled the Qin State, the Qin army killed King Yiqu of the Hun and took possession of his land. The Qin rulers also constructed walls to protect their lands from invasion by the barbarians. Before being annexed by Qin, the Zhao State maintained a powerful cavalry under the command of several famous generals that garrisoned the Zhao border. Generals of the Yan State had also led their soldiers against the Huns and defeated them several times, which forced the Hun's nomadic migration patterns to recede northwards about 500 kilometers. At the end of the Warring States Period, since the states of Qin, Yan and Zhao in the north all focused their attention on their neighbors, their defenses against the Huns weakened. The Huns exploited their weaknesses and attacked, quickly expanding their control over the land to the south of the Yinshan Mountains and the land in the Great Bend of the Yellow River.

After unification, Qin Shihuang's primary task in regard to the frontier areas was to eliminate the Hun's threat in the north. Thirty-two years after he came to the throne (215 B.C.), Qin Shihuang made an inspection tour of the northern frontier, where he witnessed firsthand the danger that the Huns presented. He then decided to send his military to rout the Hun's tribes.

At first, Li Si did not approve of sending his armies against the Huns. His reasoning was as follows: The Huns did not have permanent towns or cities that they lived in, nor did they have any accumulated wealth to guard. They were like a flock of birds, flying to and fro with great mobility that made them unpredictable, thus making them an extremely difficult enemy to defeat. If the vast Qin army went to battle with limited provisions and fodder, then

　　帝国最显著的特征就是它辽阔的土地。秦始皇统一中国之后，并不满足已有的疆土。五六年之后，国力稍有恢复，他就致力于拓展帝国的边疆。

　　秦帝国的北方是匈奴。匈奴是游牧民族，长期生活在中国北方边疆地区，擅长骑射，勇猛无比。秦朝的防卫稍有放松，匈奴人就会突入侵扰，掠夺人口和财物，造成很大的威胁。战国时期，秦、燕、赵各国都面临匈奴的威胁，特别重视应对匈奴的入侵。秦国宣太后时，秦人杀死匈奴义渠王，占领其地盘，修筑长城以阻挡匈奴的进入。赵国曾建立了一支强大的骑兵，并派名将驻守边疆。燕国的将领也曾率兵击败匈奴，使匈奴的势力范围向北退缩千余里。战国末年，北方秦、燕、赵几个诸侯国集中军事力量相互对抗，致使对匈奴的防守相对削弱。匈奴利用这个机会，迅速扩张自己的势力，占领了阴山以南和黄河河套地区的不少地方。

　　秦朝统一天下之后，消除匈奴的威胁成为北部边防的首要任务。秦始皇三十二年（公元前215年），秦始皇巡察北疆，目睹了匈奴的侵扰对北方安定造成的威胁，于是决定对匈奴用兵。

　　李斯起先并不赞同北伐匈奴。他的理由是：匈奴没有固定的城池居所，也没有需要守护的积蓄（xù），他们像鸟群一样飞来飞去，行动灵活，因而很难被制服。如果部队轻装远征，

they would have little time to drive the Huns off; if they attacked with heavy equipment and large quantities of provisions, then they would be too slow to mount an effective assault. In addition, the land that the Huns occupied was barren and infertile, and even if the Qin army could conquer them, the Hun people would be fierce subjects, and difficult to control. As Li Si felt it would be wrong to exterminate them, he spoke against wasting manpower and resources on a fight that would only exhaust them, and might even work to the benefit of the Huns.

There was some truth in Li Si's analysis, which made Qin Shihuang reconsider. At this time, an alchemist ❶ named Lu Sheng returned to Xianyang from his mission to search the sea for the Elixir of Immortality. Alchemists at that time professed the ability to perform miracles with supernatural assistance, and to help people to achieve immortality. As Qin Shihuang greatly desired immortality, he hearkened to anything that this alchemist said. Lu Sheng told him that he read in a book of augury that Qin would meet its doom because of a force called Hu. It meant that the Qin Dynasty would be destroyed by a foreign nation—the Hu. Even so, the book made no mention of who specifically the name "Hu" referred to, but according to the Qin people's interpretation, the Hu were none other than the Xiongnu, also known at the time as the Huns. Hearing his alchemist's fatalistic tale, Qin Shihuang became determined to wage war on the Huns.

Qin Shihuang ordered General Meng Tian to take 300 000 men in a campaign against the Huns. Meng Tian came from a military family; both his father and grandfather had been famous generals of the Qin State. His grandfather had earned a name for himself by taking many cities in the former states of Zhao, Wei and Han. His father, too, did the new empire a great service by leading his troops into the Chu State and capturing the king of Chu. As for Meng Tian himself, he was an experienced military leader whose skill and dedication earned him the respect of the emperor. By the emperor's order, Meng Tian led his army against the invading Huns. Before long, he recaptured the region around the Great Bend of the Yellow River and drove the Huns to the north bank of the Yellow River. The Qin army used the Yellow River as a natural barrier in the campaign, and established 44 counties along the river as fortresses against the Huns. To increase the number of Qin people in the region, Meng Tian forced many criminals to immigrate from inland China to these counties. He also built long walls along the terrain, which served as a firm barrier against the Huns for many years, and were an effective means of defending the central plains*. To guard

粮草必然不够；如果载重而行，则行动迟缓，影响作战。匈奴所据的地方土地贫瘠（jí），没有多大用处。即使俘虏了匈奴的人口，也难以控制和役使。如果把他们杀了，这不是老百姓的父母官应该做的。发动这样的战争，只会使中国疲惫，耗损人力、物力，而让匈奴称心如意。

李斯的分析不无道理，秦始皇面临着两难的选择。恰在此时，被指派到海上寻找仙药的方士❶卢生返回咸阳，方士总是声称自己掌握了各种各样神异的技术，可以使人变成神仙。秦始皇热衷于成仙，因此很相信他们的话，卢生说，有一本预言书中说："亡秦者胡也。"意思是说"消灭秦朝的人将是胡"。可是"胡"是什么，预言书中并没有说明。秦人理解，"胡"就是匈奴。于是，秦始皇决定对匈奴作战。

秦始皇派遣蒙恬率三十万大军北征匈奴。蒙恬出身于军人世家，祖父、父亲都是秦国著名的将军。祖父南征北战，攻下了赵国、魏国、韩国许多城池，战功赫（hè）赫。父亲曾率兵进攻楚国，最后俘虏了楚王。蒙恬同样转战南北，威震四方，深得秦始皇的信任。此次率兵，蒙恬很快夺取了被匈奴占领的河套地区，将匈奴逼到了黄河北岸。秦军以黄河为屏障，临河修建四十四座县城，作为防守匈奴的要塞。同时，把内地犯罪的人迁到那里以充实新设的县。蒙恬又借助地势，修筑长城。

---

❶ 方士：中国古代从事求仙等活动的人。

❶ In ancient China, an alchemist was someone who professionally prayed to the gods for blessings.

---

* central plains: the plains comprising the middle and lower reaches of the Yellow River.

the newly fortified border, Meng Tian stationed his army of 300 000 men along the Yellow River. From that time onward, the northern frontier of the Qin Empire was safe from the Huns' intrusion.

Not only did the Qin Empire expand its lands to the northern frontier, but also settled the fertile areas of the south. Qin Shihuang sent troops down to the southeastern areas of China as well as into the region of Lingnan (the area covering the present Guangdong and Guangxi provinces). The region was chiefly inhabited by people who were the natives of "Baiyue," otherwise called the people of Yue. During the Spring and Autumn Period, the people of Yue established the state of Yue with Gou Jian as the king of the state. Gou Jian was known for his firm resolve and resilience in the face of setbacks. After his armies had been defeated in a battle with the Wu State, he underwent self-imposed hardships to strengthen his character and restore his state's honor, such as sleeping on brushwood and drinking gall. Several years later, he eliminated the Wu State and annexed it into the Yue State, remaining an overlord for many years during the Spring and Autumn Period.

Lingnan was a mountainous region with dense jungles. The roads were rugged and wild animals could be found everywhere. This presented the Qin army with great difficulty in moving its supply lines. The Yue people stubbornly resisted the Qin invasion, hiding among the jungle foliage and striking them at night, soundly defeating the Qin forces.

But Qin Shihuang did not relent, and commanded that more troops be sent to Lingnan. To ensure that his supply lines were safe, he ordered the construction of a canal by Shi Lu. This canal remains to this day in Xing'an County, Guangxi Province, which is named "Lingqu Canal." In subsequent years, the Lingqu Canal allowed for water transport between northern and southern China; it also overcame the Qin army's difficulty in transporting supplies.

In 214 B.C., Qin Shihuang conquered Lingnan, thus extending the borders of the Qin Empire to the South China Sea. This laid the foundation for his controlling of China's southern frontier.

Now that Lingnan was absorbed into the unified China, the emperor built many roads between Lingnan and the other states, facilitating social and economic development in the new territory and reinforcing his administrative power, as well as improving overall communication between the north and the south. Qin Shihuang also commanded hundreds of thousands of inland people to immigrate to various places in Lingnan in order to solidify the imperial presence, causing some initial difficulties due to cultural differences between

长城成为防御匈奴、保卫中原的一道坚固的屏障。蒙恬率三十万大军沿线守卫，整个秦朝，北部边疆一直都没有受到匈奴的侵扰。

秦帝国不仅北上拓疆，而且南下开边。秦始皇派兵向中国东南部以及岭南地区（现在的广东、广西）进军。这一地区主要是越族人居住之地，称为"百越"。春秋时期，越人建立了越国，越王勾践卧薪尝胆，灭了吴国，成为春秋时代霸主之一。

岭南地区遍布山地丛林，道路崎岖（qí qū），野兽出没，交通极不方便，秦军运输粮草很困难。越族人顽强抵抗，躲藏在深山丛林，与秦军周旋，在晚上发动袭击，秦军大败。

秦始皇于是增派士兵支援岭南，又命令史禄修筑一条人工运河，作为岭南秦军的给养线，保证前线的粮草供应，这条运河就是位于现在广西兴安县的灵渠。灵渠的修建为秦军解决物资运输的困难提供了便利的条件。

公元前214年，秦始皇平定了岭南，使秦王朝的势力范围向南推到南海，奠定了中国南部疆域的基础。

秦始皇统一岭南后，为了促进这些地区的社会经济的发展，同时也为加强对这些地区的治理，派人修建了许多道路，加强南方与北方的联系。与此同时，秦始皇还从内地征发数十万民

them and the southerners. Yet they brought with them advanced technology and their cultural customs to the Yue people, and after a time, their influence contributed to rapid economic and cultural development in the Lingnan area.

众，移居岭南各地。移民确实是痛苦的事情，但客观上，内地的居民与越族人长期杂居，把内地先进的生产技术和文化传播到岭南，大大促进了当地经济文化的发展。

万里长城
The Great Wall

十 帝国工程

Chapter X Ambitious Imperial Projects

The rise of the Qin Empire was characterized by a series of ambitious construction projects, contributing to the grandiose image of Qin Shihuang's reign.

Qin Shihuang undertook many such projects, and was especially interested in accomplishing that which seemed impossible. He wished to build roads that linked all places in his empire together so that he could personally visit even the farthest reaches of his land and enjoy his own greatness at the same time.

He also focused on defending his empire from outside threats. In his mind, the empire was like one large city, and he set about enclosing it within walls that encompassed the borders of his land. This resulted in the construction of the Great Wall.

The emperor also had a passion for architecture, and aspired to build stable, long-lasting structures that would appear grandiose and majestic. His ambitions were embodied in buildings such as the Epang Palace and his future mausoleum. The grandiose and majestic architecture represented his power.

Let's have a look at these ambitious construction projects.

During the Warring States Period, the gauges for carts and chariots—the distance between two wheels on an axle—varied from state to state, as did the width of the roads. Due to differences in gauge, the carts and chariots of one state could not travel on the roads of another state, causing numerous traffic problems in the newly-unified empire. Qin Shihuang ordered a standardization of axle lengths—six *chi*—thus assuring that the carts could run smoothly along the ruts of various roads.

The emperor also built a network of roads expressly for his own carriages. He built these roads from the capital in Xianyang, and linked him to all 36 prefectures. According to historical records, these roads were 50 steps (about 69 meters) wide, but experts highly doubt that this figure is accurate. Some historians hold it to be a mistake in the record, and that the actual width was 50 *chi* (about 11.5 meters). The roads were smooth and firm, with the middle part slightly higher than the sides, and with pine trees planted on both sides of the road at 6.9 meter intervals. These roads extended in all directions, and were based on roads already present in the former states, although the emperor broadened and improved them. One section in the center of each road was reserved for carriages of the emperor, or those of other prominent princes and nobles. Officials, messengers and other travelers were only allowed on the sides of the road, although in some remote areas the imperial road was placed

帝国就是一座大厦。它的兴起总是伴随着浩大工程的建设，巨大的建筑往往成为帝国最直观的形象。

秦始皇热衷于建设，而且是建造那些最初看起来简直无法实现的工程。他热衷于建设道路，为的是把帝国的每个部分现实地连接起来，为的是能够走遍自己看管的每一寸土地，在亲身体验帝国雄伟的同时，也感受自己的伟大。

他热衷于国家的防卫工程。他想象着帝国就是一座巨大的城市，如果有可能他将用高大的城墙将整个帝国围护起来，事实上，他已经用万里长城捍卫着自己的王朝。

他热衷于建筑。他渴望宏伟、坚固、永恒的建筑，于是修建阿房（ē páng）宫以及自己未来的陵墓。壮丽雄伟的建筑代表了他的权力。

让我们来看看这些浩大的工程。

战国时期，各诸侯国的车轨不同，道路的宽度也不一样。所谓车轨，就是车子两轮之间的距离。车轨不同，意味着一个国家的车子在另一个国家可能无法通行。这给统一后的秦帝国的交通带来了不便。秦始皇因此下令，车轨皆宽六尺，修造的车子统一车轮宽度，这样就可以在各地行驶。

秦朝修建有一种特别的道路——驰道，它是皇帝乘车出行的道路。驰道以首都咸阳为中心向四面辐射，遍布全国三十六个郡。据记载，驰道路面宽50步，约69米。这个数字显然太大，专家认为记载可能有差错，或许是50尺，约11.5米宽。路面中心稍高，平坦坚实；路两旁种植松树，间隔为6.9米左右。秦朝四通八达的驰道大部分是在原有道路的基础上扩建而成的，路的一条通道或者中央通道专供皇帝、显赫的王公贵族的车辆行驶，官员、信使和其他人只准在路侧的边道上行走。但在远离京城、偏僻的地方，御用道路与普通道路恐怕就合而为一了。

directly over ordinary roads. Historians estimate that the entire network of imperial roads extended over 6 800 kilometers.

Thirty-five years after he came to the throne (212 B.C.), Qin Shihuang instructed General Meng Tian to build a "straight" road from Xianyang up to the north so that he could tour the entire country. This road started in Yunyang, northwest of Xianyang, and ran all the way to the county town of Jiuyuan (west of Baotou City, in the present Inner Mongolia Autonomous Region). The road was called "the straight road," perhaps owing to the fact that it led directly to the capital. It took Meng Tian and his men about two and a half years to finish the construction of the road, but once they had finished, the road was over 600 kilometers long. Considering that the whole road was built over barren hills and mountains, and that half of the road traversed the Ziwuling Area (in the present northern Shaanxi Province) and a vast stretch of desert (in the present Inner Mongolia Autonomous Region), the project was difficult and time-consuming. As the road meandered through mountains and rivers, the builders had to raze the mountain tops and level the deep valleys. It is said that if someone took the earth dug for the road to build a wall one meter high and one meter wide, then that wall would encircle half of the earth. It was during his fifth tour of the country that Qin Shihuang died of illness in Shaqiu (the present county of Pingxiang, Hebei Province), and the imperial carriages who carried his remains back to Xianyang used this very road.

During the time of the Roman Empire, whenever the Romans conquered an area, they would build roads that connected that area to the rest of the empire, hence the proverb "All roads lead to Rome." The roads that Qin Shihuang constructed during his reign were perhaps even wider than those of the Romans, and due to his similar achievement in linking the unified nation with a series of roads, it could be said of the Qin Dynasty that "All roads lead to Xianyang." Even if these roads were only 50 *chi* (11.5 meters) broad, they still surpassed those of the Romans, few of which exceeded the width of 8.5 meters. ❶

The roads constructing during the reign of the Qin Emperor greatly influenced later dynasties, and established a general pattern for roads in China thereafter.

Another symbol of the Qin Dynasty's ambitious projects is the Great Wall.

When Qin Shihuang ordered his people to build the Great Wall, it was

这些道路，有些至今仍然可以通行。专家粗略地估计，秦帝国公路的总长度约为6 800公里。

秦始皇三十五年（公元前212年），为了游历天下，秦始皇命蒙恬将军主持开通一条从咸阳北上的"直道"。这条直道从咸阳西北面的云阳，直达九原郡城（今内蒙古自治区包头市西）。大概是由于"直达"的缘故，故称"直道"。大约修了两年半的时间，全长1 800里（600千米）。这条道路是在荒山野岭之中修建的，约有一半的道路穿过陕西省北部的子午岭，还要通过今内蒙古自治区的大片沙漠，其难度可想而知。一般山路都是依山傍水，蜿蜒（wān yán）而行，但为了建成所谓的"直道"，施工者不得不开山填谷，将山头削去，填平深谷，从而保持道路的径直、平坦。有人粗略地估算过，直道工程所取用的土方，如果堆筑成高一米、宽一米的土墙，可以绕地球半圈。秦始皇第五次东巡、北上，最后病逝于沙丘（在今河北省平乡县），载着秦始皇遗体的车队就是经由这条直道返回咸阳的。

罗马帝国每征服一个地区，就会修筑大道，有所谓"条条大路通罗马"的成语。秦王朝修建道路，也形成了"条条大道通咸阳"的局面。秦代的道路可能比罗马大道宽。专家认为，秦道宽如果是50尺，也有11.5米宽，而罗马大道很少超过8.5米。❶

秦帝国的交通线路网对后世影响很大，基本奠定了后来全中国主要道路的总体格局。

秦代伟大工程的另一个标志是长城。

秦始皇下令修筑长城的时候，一定没有意识到长城在现代

---

❶ 参见［英］崔瑞德、鲁惟一，《剑桥中国秦汉史》，汉译本，中国社会科学出版社1992年，第119页。

❶ See p. 119 in *The Cambridge History of China*, Vol. 1: *The Ch' in and Han Empires,* 221 B.C.~A.D. 220 by Denis C. Twitchett, Chinese version published by China Social Science Press in 1992.

unlikely that he expected this wall to later become a Chinese national symbol. Although he was not the first ruler to commission the building of defensive walls, he is known for the large-scale walls that were constructed during his reign.

During the Warring States Period, the Qin, Zhao and Yan states all constructed extensive fortifications along their northern borders to defend against the Huns. The length of these walls in the Zhao State alone was over 650 kilometers. In 213 B.C., Qin Shihuang charged General Meng Tian with the daunting task of constructing new fortifications in the north to further prevent incursions from the Huns. Under Meng Tian's leadership, several hundreds of thousands of workers began to build a new wall upon the fortifications originally built by the former Qin, Zhao and Yan states. The new wall took them over four years to complete. Starting from Lintao in the west, the Great Wall of the Qin Dynasty passed through the modern day provinces of Gansu, Ningxia, Shanxi, Inner Mongolia, Hebei and Liaoning, ending in Korea in the east. The wall was more than 10 000 *li* (5000 kilometers) in length, thus earning it the name that Chinese use to refer to it: "The long wall of 10 000 *li*." The Great Wall was the most impressive fortification built during the Qin Dynasty. What makes it even more remarkable is that people with simple tools and poor means of transportation could complete such a monumental project in such a short time. The wall was mostly made by stamping earth and gravel, and was ingeniously shaped to fit the landscape it covered. The wall proceeded along lofty, cragged mountains and looked spectacular and magnificent. Watchtowers and fortresses were built along the wall at regular intervals in high and steep areas, or at important mountain passes. The construction of the Great Wall displays the Qin Empire's uncanny efficiency in mobilizing and organizing the people to complete a task of peculiar strategic and symbolic importance.

Once the wall was completed, soldiers kept vigilant watch over the Qin border with the Huns, resulting in more than a decade without war between the Empire and the Hun tribes. This provided sufficient protection for the country's heartland, and fostered increased economic and cultural development.

The Great Wall now stands as a wonder of the world, but at the time, its construction placed a heavy burden upon the Qin people, draining them of manpower and resources. This manpower not only consisted of the 300 000 soldiers that accompanied General Meng Tian, but also included the conscripted workers and exiled convicts who worked on the wall, which at

会成为中国的象征。秦始皇并不是第一个修筑长城的人，但长城万里的规模却是在他的手中形成。

战国时期，为了防御匈奴，秦、赵、燕都分别在自己的北部边境建造长城，其中赵国的长城长达一千三百多里（650千米）。公元前213年，秦始皇命令大将蒙恬负责修建新长城。蒙恬率领数十万民众在秦、赵、燕旧长城的基础上，用了四年的时间，完成了新长城的修筑。秦长城西起临洮（táo），经过今天的甘肃、宁夏、陕西、内蒙古、河北、辽宁等省，东至朝鲜，全长一万多里，号称"万里长城"。它无疑是秦帝国最浩大的边防工程。在当时工具简陋、交通不便的条件下，仅用数年就完成如此浩大的工程，实在难以想象。整个长城顺应不同的地形地貌，蜿蜒起伏，气势雄伟，用土、土石和沙石混筑而成。险峻之处建有城堡，每相隔一段距离设有关卡。整个工程充分显示出秦王朝强大的组织能力和军事工程学上的卓越成就。

万里长城建造完工，沿线有士卒把守。秦朝与匈奴之间十几年没有发生战争。长城的建造保卫了中原地区经济、文化的发展。

被誉为世界奇迹的万里长城，其工程需要投入的人力、物力十分巨大，整个建造过程给广大人民带来了沉重的负担。修筑长城的劳动力除了蒙恬率领的三十万大军，还有从附近征发的民众和被发配边疆的罪犯，人数最多时可能达到五十万。其

some points reached a total of nearly 500 000 people. As most of the wall was built over dangerous mountain areas that lacked proper roads, the working conditions were poor and the workload tiresome and difficult. Many workers died of exhaustion or illness, and others were severely wounded during the arduous labor. The building of the Great Wall took so many men away from the inner territories that sometimes only women were available to bring provisions up to the workers when they ran short.

Cries of discontent over the project arose throughout the empire, generating legends such as the story of Meng Jiang's bitter cry over the Great Wall.

According to the myth, a man named Wan Xiliang hid in a garden to escape being drafted into working on the Great Wall. Inside the garden, he met a young woman named Meng Jiang, and they fell in love at first sight, marrying one another soon thereafter. But they had only been married for three days when Wan Xiliang was caught and sent to work on the Great Wall. Over the subsequent years, Meng Jiang missed her husband day and night, but received no word of him. When winter came, Meng Jiang worried that her husband would freeze during his work, so she made him a set of cotton-padded clothes and set off to find him. Her journey was fraught with peril and tribulation, but her love for her husband drove her on, until she reached the Great Wall, where she searched in vain for Wan Xiliang. Finally, she found someone who knew him—but he told her that Wan Xiliang had died from exhaustion some time ago, and was buried at the foot of the Great Wall. Distraught, Meng Jiang wept and wailed so bitterly that Heaven pitied her. With a tremendous crack, a 400 kilometer-long section of the Great Wall collapsed, allowing Meng Jiang to recover her husband's body.

The myth of Meng Jiang reflects the people's feelings at the time about the suffering and burdens that the construction of the Great Wall brought upon them.

Another momentous project was Qin Shihuang's construction of the Lingqu Canal, which was built to allow him to conquer the Lingnan region. The Lingqu Canal links two rivers together: the Xiang River that flows into the Yangtze, and the Li River that flows into the Pearl River. One of the oldest canals in China, the Lingqu Canal connected two major waterways and aided in Qin's expansion to the southwest. Although initially constructed for military purposes, its design is as effective for general transport as China's other two famous canals, the Dujiangyan Irrigation System in Sichuan and the Zhengguo Canal in Shanxi. For more than two millennia, this canal has played an important role in local

地偏僻险要，劳动条件极为恶劣，军民伤亡病死惨重，男人不够，甚至妇女也被动员去送粮草。

民间百姓怨声载道，流传着孟姜女哭长城的故事：

传说万喜良因为逃避修筑长城的苦役，藏到了孟姜女家的花园中，看到了孟姜女，两人一见钟情，于是成婚。可是结婚刚刚三天，万喜良又被征调到修筑长城的工地。孟姜女日思夜想，可万喜良却一连几年都没有音讯。冬天到了，孟姜女担心丈夫无法忍受北方的寒冷，便带着缝制好的棉衣去长城工地寻找。孟姜女历尽千辛万苦，终于来到长城脚下，却找不到万喜良的踪影。后来，经多方打听，得知丈夫已经活活累死了，被葬在长城下面。孟姜女悲痛欲绝，放声大哭，哭声感天动地。突然一声巨响，八百里长城倒下了，露出了万喜良的尸骨。

孟姜女哭倒长城的情节显然出于虚构，但建造长城给许多家庭带来巨大痛苦，增加了民众的负担，引起普通老百姓的强烈不满，却是事实。

另外，值得一提的还有秦始皇开拓岭南时修筑的灵渠。灵渠把湘江和漓江的水连接起来，沟通了珠江和长江两大水系，虽然是为军事目的修建的，但它设计精妙，与四川都江堰、陕西郑国渠齐名，是最古老的运河之一。两千多年来，对中国的

irrigation, as well as transportation between northern and southern China.

Qin Shihuang also commissioned two projects solely for himself: his palace and his mausoleum.

King Xiao of the Qin State was the first to choose Xianyang as the Qin capital. In the successive reigns of the following six kings, the capital became increasingly majestic; even before the unification of China under the Qin, Xianyang was already a famous and prosperous city. While the Qin armies were busy conquering the other states to unify China, Qin Shihuang was building palaces and gardens to beautify his capital city.

During the Qin conquest, whenever he annexed a new state, Qin Shihuang would order a new palace built at a place in Xianyang called "Beiban." Each palace thus constructed was modeled in the style of the palace of the annexed state. Facing the Wei River to the south, Beiban contained many palaces with long corridors, pavilions, terraces and open halls, all linked to one another. The emperor brought back the beauties treasures and artifacts he took from the other states to the Beiban palaces, displaying them to the people as a way to flaunt his great military triumphs.

Aside from the Beiban palaces, Qin Shihuang also constructed many other palaces around the main imperial palace in Xianyang.

Twenty-seven years after he came to the throne (220 B.C.), Qin Shihuang had another palace built by the south bank of the Wei River. The palace was first called the Xin Palace, but was later renamed "The Temple of the Celestial Pole" as a symbol of Polaris, the north star. The name derives from a Confucian saying recorded in *Analects: On Studying* that states: "He who exercises government by means of virtue is like the north polar star in its place, around which all of the stars revolve in homage." The ancient Chinese held that among the celestial bodies, the north star lay at the center and all of the other stars revolved around it. For this reason, the north star was regarded as the most honorable star, and therefore The Temple of the Celestial Pole symbolized the supreme status of the imperial family. A road from this temple led to Lishan Mountain, and the front hall of the temple had a sweet spring surrounding it. There was also a paved path from the temple that led all the way to Xianyang, an enclosed walkway with walls on both sides. When the emperor walked along this path, he was invisible to people outside of the walls.

Aside from these palaces, Qin Shihuang also had many "xinggong" and "ligong" built. In ancient China, a "xinggong" was a palace that the emperor stayed in during short visits to a city, while a "ligong" was the palace that the

南北交通发挥了极大作用，至今当地的农业灌溉仍在利用灵渠。

秦始皇有两类工程是为自己修建的，这就是宫殿与陵墓。

秦国自秦孝公定都咸阳以来，经过六代君主的建设，都城已经具有相当规模。秦统一前，咸阳已经成为闻名天下的繁荣都市。随着统一战争的节节胜利，秦始皇不断扩建他的宏伟帝都，大兴宫殿园林。

秦始皇在兼并六国时，每吞灭一个诸侯，就命人仿照该国的宫殿样式，在咸阳的北阪建筑一处新的宫殿。北阪南临渭水，在它附近，宫殿长廊亭台楼阁相连，让人应接不暇。从六国所得的美女、宝物，便存放在这些宫殿中。秦始皇以这种特殊的方式炫耀其伟大的军事胜利。

除六国宫殿以外，秦始皇还以咸阳宫为中心兴建了大批宫殿。

秦始皇二十七年（公元前220年），在渭河以南建造信宫，又改名为极庙，"象天极"，即象征天上的北极星。《论语·为政》中载孔子说："为政以德，譬如北辰居其所而众星共之。"意思是说，用德来治理国家，就像北极星一样，处在自己的位置上，其他星辰都会环绕着它。中国古人认为北极星居于天体的中央，为众星所环绕，在星辰中最为尊贵，因此极庙象征着皇室的尊贵地位。极庙有道路通向骊山，建有甘泉前殿。又建甬道，与咸阳相通。甬道是全封闭的道路，两侧砌墙，皇帝从中间通行，外人看不到。

秦始皇还兴建了许多行宫和离宫。行宫、离宫是皇帝外出

emperor spent the summer or winter in. Many such palaces can be found around the north and south banks of the Wei River. One man named Jia Shan from the West Han Dynasty wrote, "While traveling westward from Xiangyang to Yong County, there are as many as 300 summer and winter palaces along the way." This number may have been exaggerated, but the fact remains that many palaces surrounded Xianyang. Some believed that these palaces corresponded to the stars in the sky: At the center of these other palaces, the Palace at Xianyang symbolized the Ziwei star and the emperor's dwelling place. Flowing through the city of Xianyang, the Wei River was regarded as the galaxy in the sky. The arch bridge which linked the north and south parts of the city was thought to correspond to the Altair, a binary star, and the palaces surrounding were like the clusters of stars in the heaven. Due to the deliberate layout of the palaces, proper maintenance, and an impressive architectural style, these palaces projected a fitting image of the Qin Emperor: magnificent, grandiose and extravagant.

Yet even these palaces could not satisfy the emperor; he believed that Xianyang was overpopulated and that the palaces built by the previous kings were too small. In his opinion, a place called Shangling Yuan, located on the south bank of the Wei River between the cities of Feng and Hao, which were the former capitals of Kings Wen and Wu of the Zhou Dynasty, was "a place fit for an emperor" and would be the perfect place to build his imperial palace. Therefore, in the 35th year of his reign (212 B.C.), at age 48, Qin Shihuang gave the order to forcibly recruit 700 000 workers, some to build the new complex of imperial palaces in Shangling Yuan, and the rest to construct his mausoleum on Lishan Mountain.

According to the design specifications, the imperial palaces at Shangling Yuan constituted a massive architectural project. The first palace that the appointed workers attempted to build was the Epang Palace. While historical sources remain unclear, there are several explanations for this odd name, Epang. Some believe that its name comes from its proximity to the capital; others believe its name came from its spaciousness; still others believe that because the palace was built by a high mountain, that "Epang" meant "high." At any rate, the Epang Palace was gargantuan for a single building, and even though the people spent three years working on it, after the emperor died, the palace remained incomplete. In addition, the emperor's death three years after commissioning the project also halted construction on any of the other palaces.

The Epang Palace was 500 steps from east to west and 50 *zhang** from

巡游时的临时住所。这些宫殿在渭河南北两岸有不少。西汉贾山说：从咸阳向西，直到雍县，"离宫三百"。这个数据很可能有夸张，但咸阳一带形成了一个庞大的宫殿群应该是事实。人们以为，咸阳宫殿与天上星体有某种对应的关系。咸阳宫位居中央，象征紫微星，是帝王所居的地方。渭河从咸阳城中流过，象征天上的银河，连接南北的拱桥则是天上的牵牛星，周围的诸多宫殿则是满天繁星。这些宫殿大多气势雄伟，布局严整，错落有致，一派帝都壮丽雄伟、富丽堂皇的景象。

然而，秦始皇仍不满足。他以为咸阳人多，先王所建的宫殿太小。渭河以南的上林苑位于周文王的都城丰和周武王的都城镐（hào）之间，秦始皇认为这里是"帝王之都"，是修建帝王宫殿的最佳地方。秦始皇三十五年（公元前212年），他四十八岁，下令征发七十万人分别在上林苑修建朝宫，在骊山建造陵墓。

朝宫的设计规模极其庞大，秦人计划先建朝宫的前殿——阿房宫。为什么称做"阿房"，后人解释不一。一说是靠近咸阳的意思；一说是因为宫殿宽大；一说是在高山的旁边，有高大的意思。仅仅是阿房宫的规模就相当大了，建造了三年，直到秦始皇去世，阿房宫还未建好，更不用说计划建造的朝宫了。

阿房宫"东西五百步，南北五十丈，上可以坐万人，下可以

---

*　1 *zhang* = 3.3m.

south to north, with a capacity of holding 10 000 people and a height of 5 *zhang*. It was said that the palace gate was made of magnets, and that when foreign envoys came to pay tribute before the emperor, if they had carried weapons with them, the weapons would be caught by the gate. The emperor also hoped that if this happened, the envoys would be alarmed, and believe that gods were present, and were protecting the Qin Dynasty.

Around the Epang Palace, various channels led to roads that ran from the palace gate southward to Zhongnan Mountain. At the top of the mountain was a "que," a huge column-shaped building used as a watchtower in front of the palace gate, meaning that the entrance to the palace was at the top of Zhongnan Mountain. Another bridge-like channel led to Xianyang, crossing the the Wei River from the Epang Palace and leading northward.

In Epang Village today, a huge earthen platform is still visible, 400 meters from east to west, 110 meters from south to north, and 15 meters high. The local people call the platform "Shi Huang's Platform to Heaven." According to legend, due to Qin Shihuang's wish for immortality, he ordered Xu Fu to find the Elixir of Life by sailing the sea in search of Mount Penglai, the abode of the Eight Immortals. He was so anxious to receive the elixir that he built this high platform along the Epang Palace so that he could look out and see Xu Fu as soon as he returned. Yet Qin Shihuang died of illness before the Epang Palace was completed; to mock his search for immortality, people of later ages called this platform "The Platform of Vain Hope."

The Epang Palace also housed many women, all wives or maids of the kings or princes of the former six states. Every day, they dressed carefully, and put on makeup that they believed would please the emperor, hoping to attract his attention. As many as 10 000 such women lived here, yet most of them never had the opportunity to meet the emperor in the 36 years of his rule.

The Epang Palace is a case study in extravagance. Archeologists have discovered many elaborate artifacts in its ruins, such as eaves tiles, earthenware pipes for drainage, floor tiles, and hollow bricks. Patterns on the eaves tiles depict images of life, such as flowers, insects, birds and animals. The unearthed hollow bricks feature prominent patterns of flying phoenixes and dragons. The walls are covered in beautiful paintings of people, animals, plants and buildings, all in vivid colors. These evidences only give a hint of the original majesty of this ornate imperial palace.

But the beauty of the Epang Palace came at the expense of the people, causing a backlash of negative sentiment from the masses. A saying that

建五丈旗"。传说，殿门用磁石做成，又称磁石门。外族使者来朝贡时，从此门进入，如果携带兵器，便会被磁石门吸住。使者遇到这种情况，往往大惊失色，以为秦朝有神灵相助，更生敬畏之心。

阿房宫四周建有架空的阁道，从殿门向南通过阁道可直接到达终南山，在终南山顶修建"阙（què）"，是一种表示宫门的立柱，这意味着秦始皇所建的宫殿大门在终南山顶。从阿房宫开始，向北修建一种与天桥相似的"复道"，横跨渭水，通向咸阳。

如今在阿房村南，有一座巨大的土台基，东西400米，南北110米，高约15米，当地老百姓称为"始皇上天台"。传说，秦始皇希望自己长生不老，便令徐市渡海去求长生不老之药。秦始皇盼望心切，于是在阿房宫内筑起高台登望。阿房宫尚未完工，秦始皇便病死于出巡的途中。后人讥笑秦始皇，把这个土台称为"妄想台"。

阿房宫内住满了原六国的嫔妃、宫女，她们日夜对镜梳妆，个个都以皇帝的喜好而梳装打扮，希望得到皇帝的宠幸。秦始皇的后宫女子达一万多人，有的在宫中三十六年都不曾见过皇帝一面。

阿房宫极尽奢侈豪华，考古人员在阿房宫遗址发现了大量瓦当、陶制排水管道、铺地砖、空心砖等。瓦当上的图纹有各种花虫鸟兽，出土的空心砖上有龙凤纹，龙凤飞舞，若腾空在天。在遗址的墙面上，还发现了大量的壁画，有人物、动物、植物、建筑等，色彩极为丰富，足见当时宫殿的华美绮（qǐ）丽。

如此大规模地兴建宫殿，导致民众怨声载道。当时流传着

reflects this sentiment was spread across the land: "Epang, Epang, Shihuang goes down." In a way, the construction of the Epang Palace was a catalyst for the fall of the Qin Dynasty. After Qin Shihuang died, his son succeeded him as the second Qin Emperor (called Qin Ershi), and he continued the construction of the frivolously extravagant palace. Not long after, rebel armies under the command of Xiang Yu and others overthrew the Qin Dynasty. When these armies took the city of Xianyang, they set fire to the Epang Palace and the buildings surrounding it, burning them to ashes. Some claimed that the fires among the palace's ashes continued to burn for over three months afterward.

The ancient Chinese believed in the immortality of the soul. They held that when a man died, his soul would live on in another world; therefore, graves were significant to them, especially the graves of their emperors. Ancient graves lacked mounds, but around the Spring and Autumn Period, mounds on graves appeared, on which trees were planted. As a general rule, the larger a grave was, the higher the mound was, and the more trees were planted there. They believed that the more funerary goods the deceased had in his grave, the higher position he had occupied in his mortal life. Graves became symbols of power—and Qin Shihuang's mausoleum was a massive construction project, overshadowing the mausoleums of all other emperors in China's history.

Qin Shihuang's mausoleum is located near the village of Xia He, which is five kilometers to the east of the county of Lintong in Shaanxi Province, bordered by Lishan Mountain on the north and the Wei River on the south. It is also called "Lishan Mausoleum." The construction of the mausoleum began as early as Qin Shihuang's initial ascension to the throne in the original Qin State, and production increased dramatically in his later years. It is believed that hundreds of thousands of workers contributed to its construction, and it was so large and involved that the mausoleum was not even completed by the time of the emperor's death. His son and successor, Qin Ershi, completed the mausoleum two years after his death, 39 years after construction began.

Qin Shihuang had several reasons for building his mausoleum at the foot of Lishan Mountain. It is said that the mountains to the south of the Wei River looks like a gigantic dragon, with Lishan Mountain as its head and Huashan Mountain as its body, and its tail is several hundred kilometers long, winding all the way to the area of Tongguan in Shaanxi Province. Built at the foot of the mountain, Lishan Mausoleum serves as the actual head of this gigantic dragon. With its original height of about 116 meters and a base of 485 meters long and 515 meters wide, Lishan Mausoleum looks like an upside-down

这样一首民谣："阿房，阿房，亡始皇。"阿房宫的建设，从某种意义上说，加速了秦王朝的灭亡。秦始皇病逝后，秦二世继续修建阿房宫。当试图推翻秦朝统治的项羽率军队攻入咸阳时，一把大火，焚烧了阿房宫。据说，大火熊熊燃烧了三个多月才熄灭。

中国古人相信灵魂不灭，以为人死后，灵魂仍生活在另一个世界里，因此对古人而言，墓葬非常重要，帝王的墓葬更是不同一般。早期的墓葬没有封土，即墓的上面没有土堆。大约春秋时期，墓上开始有封土，封土上植树。通常情况下，陵墓越大，封土越高，陵墓上种植的树木越多，墓内的陪葬品数量越多，说明墓主人的身份地位越显贵。陵墓显然成为权力的象征。秦始皇陵规模巨大，堪称中国古代帝王陵墓之最。

秦始皇的帝陵位于今陕西省西安市临潼（tóng）县以东五公里的下河村附近，北靠骊山，南临渭河，又称骊山陵。秦王即位时便开始营造骊山陵墓，晚年更是加紧修建，陵墓工地施工人数最多时可能有几十万。他去世时，陵墓还未完工，秦二世又用了两年的时间才建成，前后历时三十九年。

秦始皇为什么把帝陵建在骊山脚下？据说，渭河以南的山脉，像一条巨龙，骊山是龙头，华山是龙身，龙尾蜿蜒数百里，直至陕西省潼关一带。骊山陵建在龙头上，成为巨龙之首。骊山陵是一个口向下的方形巨斗（dǒu），原高五十多丈，约116米，陵基东西长485米，南北宽约515米。经过两千多年的风雨

bucket. Over two millennia, the mausoleum has suffered erosion from the weather as well as vandalism. It now stands as a giant pyramid of earth, 76 meters high and 345 meters long and 330 wide at the base, covering a total of 56 square kilometers. In the mausoleum, there are two ramparts which serve as the symbolic separation between the imperial city and the capital city. The inner city is in the shape of a square with a circumference of 3 890 meters, while the outer city is in the shape of a rectangle, whose circumference is 6 294 meters.

According to historical records, the grave inside the Lishan Mausoleum was dug so deep that it reached ground water. To keep the spring water from flowing out, the ground was cast in copper before the coffin was placed into the grave. The whole underground palace was filled with rare jewels and precious stones; stone sculptures of officials stood in two lines according to their ranks. A mural of the constellations in the night sky was painted on the dome of this underground palace, and pearls dotted the scene, representing the sun, moon and stars. On the ground was a representation of the territory and terrain of the Qin Empire, including the 100 rivers and the land of ancient China. The rivers were made of mercury, flowing by the command of a mechanical device. To ensure that the tomb was as bright as the real world, craftsmen made statue-like candles with the grease of sharks. Each of these candle statues had a bright pearl called "huo zhu" in its mouth, so that even if the statues burned out, the pearls could still give off light. Crossbow traps were rigged throughout the tomb to protect it from grave robbers. Trees were also planted on the top of the mausoleum, making it appear to be an ordinary hill.

In 1982, a group of scientists sent probes deep into the soil around the tomb, employing modern technology to detect trace amounts of mercury. The probes revealed abnormally high quantities of mercury, some 100 times the naturally occurring rate, in an area of 1 200 square meters around Qin Shihuang's mausoleum. Some geologists think that the unusually large amount of mercury comes from the underground palace, which indicates that there are indeed large quantities of mercury in the mausoleum. From this we can infer that the people of the time attained a high level of skill in extracting mercury from other materials. Apart from mercury, many copper arrows have also been found around the tomb.

In the 37th year of his reign (210 B.C.), Qin Shihuang, died of an illness at age 50 while touring eastern China. His chariots came back to Xianyang via the "straight road," and in September of this year, the emperor was buried in his mausoleum at Lishan Mountain. His son and successor Qin

侵蚀和人为破坏，至今还保存有高76米、东西长345米、南北宽330米的夯（hāng）土堆。秦始皇陵园和随葬的范围，总面积达56平方公里。陵园筑有两道城墙，象征着皇城和都城。内城为正方形，周长3 890米；外城为长方形，周长6 294米。

据史料记载，骊山陵墓的墓室一直挖到地下水的深度，然后用铸铜浇灌，防止泉水上溢，再将棺木放置其中。整个地宫放满了珍奇珠宝，石头雕刻的百官按照职位的高低排列在两边。地宫的穹顶画天文星宿之图，用珍珠宝石筑成日月星辰，下面是百川和九州的缩略图，用水银模仿江河大海，以机械方式令其流动不息，以此来表示大秦帝国的疆域形势。为了让陵墓中像人间一样充满光明，工匠用鲛鱼油做成玉像，玉像口衔火珠，以求长久不灭。为了防范偷盗，宫殿四周布满了可自动射箭的机关，一旦盗墓者进入墓穴，就会触动机关，自动射出弩箭。在陵墓上面种有树木，看上去与自然形成的山丘没有什么区别。

1982年，科学家利用现代微量汞的探测技术，在秦始皇帝陵附近发现1 200平方米的汞异常区。地质学家认为，汞异常是来自地宫的内部，表明秦始皇陵中的确存在大量的水银，足见当时中国的汞提炼技术已达到了相当高的水平。另外，在陵墓附近还发现了大量的铜矢。

秦始皇三十七年（公元前210年），秦始皇五十岁，病逝于东巡的途中。车队从直道回到了咸阳。这一年九月，秦始皇被安葬在骊山。秦二世说："先王后宫的女子，凡是没有生育的，

Ershi said, "Some concubines of the late emperor did not give birth to any of his children, and thus it would be inappropriate for them to leave the palace and become other men's wives." By his order, all of these women were buried alive in the tomb with the emperor. He also ordered that all of the workers who took part in the construction of the underground tomb be executed, as well as anyone who might reveal secrets about the traps or treasures inside, totaling nearly 10 000 people.

For more than two thousand years, this magnificent mausoleum with a vast trove of treasures has attracted a great deal of attention. Many later dynasties guarded it carefully, but it was also raided and damaged several times. One such time was shortly after the emperor's death. In 207 B.C., three years after Qin Ershi came to the throne, when Xiang Yu was burning the Epang Palace, he also set Lishan Mausoleum on fire. He then ordered 300 000 people to mine the mausoleum for treasures, and for an entire month, these men looted many treasures from the mausoleum. There are still two deep ditches around Qin Shihuang's mausoleum today, one on the south and another on the north, called the "Ditches of Ba Wang" by the local people. It is believed that Xiang Yu commanded their creation to facilitate ransacking the mausoleum.

Stories from the Han Dynasty illustrate that Qin Shihuang's mausoleum was left in in a poor state at that time. According to a story, one day, a shepherd boy came here with his flocks, and one of his sheep accidentally fell into a gaping hole. The boy walked into the tomb to look for his sheep with a torch, but out of his carelessness, he caused a fire in the tomb, burning some of what was left. Another story states that south of the mausoleum lived an elderly man, who discovered a massive smooth stone when he was digging a well. In order to find out what was under the stone, the villagers selected two strong men from among themselves and sent them to the bottom of the hole with torches. When the two men returned, they told the other villagers that when they had reached the bottom, they had found an immense cavern, with numerous women in beautiful attire lying everywhere with stone stools lying beside them. They also found a large number of copper utensils. Believing that they had come across with ghosts, the villagers hastily covered the hole with the massive stone. This story remains to this day in the area of Xi' an City in Shaanxi Province.

Despite the abuse the mausoleum has suffered over the centuries, due to the vertical shaft structure and the great depth of the mausoleum, all of the treasures in the underground palace, as well as those in Qin Shihuang's coffin, remain intact. People today still seek to discover the secrets of this vast tomb.

不适合再放出宫去。"于是，下令将秦始皇的那些嫔（pín）妃全部活埋在墓中。秦二世又唯恐施工的工匠和一些知情者泄露陵墓中的机关和宝藏的秘密，在封闭墓道中门之后，又迅速落下墓道外门，将这些人也统统活埋在地宫中，死者近万人。

两千多年来，这一规模宏大、宝藏丰富的陵墓无疑吸引了众多目光的注视，既受到历代王朝的保护，也遭到多次盗掘和破坏。实际上，秦始皇陵刚刚封上，就遭到了最大的破坏。秦二世三年（公元前207年），项羽在烧毁阿房宫的同时，也火烧骊山陵园，并派三十万人挖掘陵墓，搬运随葬的珠宝，一连搬了三十多天还未搬完。在秦始皇陵的南面和西北面各有一条深沟，当地人称之为"霸王沟"，据说就是当年项羽所挖。

传说汉朝的时候，秦始皇陵已经荒芜，有个牧童来这里放羊，羊不小心掉进了一个洞穴中，牧童于是举着火把进墓寻找，不小心失火，焚烧了一些东西。还有一个更神奇的故事，说陵墓南部有一个七十岁的老人在打井时发现了一块光滑的大石板，于是召集村人把它掀开，露出了一个极深的洞穴。村里挑选了两个强壮的男子打着火把下去打探，两人上来后，说这个洞穴看不到边际，里面倒卧着许多衣着美丽的女子，四周摆放着很多石凳，还有很多铜质器物。村里人以为遇到了鬼魂，急忙向洞中撒些石灰，又将大石板盖上。这个故事至今还流传在陕西省西安一带。

秦始皇陵在两千多年的岁月中，遭到有意无意的破坏，损失是巨大的，然而由于陵墓内部是竖穴式的，地宫较深，所以地宫内的文物及秦始皇的棺木应该说仍完好无损。直到今天，人们一直期待着揭开秦始皇陵的秘密。

One of the most memorable and oft-mentioned features of Qin Shihuang's tomb is the presence of the terracotta warriors and horses buried along with him.

Xiyang Village is a village near Qin Shihuang's mausoleum. It is said that when the people of this village were digging for a well, they frequently found earthenware pots in the ground, which they called "Pots from the Lords of Pottery." Finding this pottery bothered them, though, as they feared they had dug their well on the site of an ancient temple, so they hung the pots in trees and smashed them. As it so happened, a man who was in the area to inspect the well learned of this discovery of pottery and immediately reported it to the government. The officials in charge of cultural preservation sent a representative to collect pieces of the pots and restore them. Then, in 1974, the State Administration of Cultural Heritage organized a team called "the archaeological excavation team for the pits of the terracotta warriors and horses in Qin Shihuang's mausoleum," and excavation began at the site of the tomb. They worked for nearly two years and finally found three large pits 1.5 kilometers east of Qin Shihuang's burial ground where a large number of terracotta warriors and horses were buried with the emperor.

According to the order of their discoveries, the three pits are tagged Pit 1, Pit 2, and Pit 3, and the total area of the three pits is 22 780 square meters. Pit 1 is a rectangular pit, about 230 meters long, 62 meters wide, and 5 meters deep, with a total area of 14 260 square meters. On the eastern side of the pit stand 210 terracotta warriors in three arrays, facing east. All of these terracotta warriors are life-sized; some of them are dressed in robes and others are depicted wearing armor. The terracotta warriors vary in facial expression, uniform, and style of armor, and look remarkably lifelike. On the southern and northern sides of the pit stand two arrays of armored warriors, facing south and north respectively. Pit 1 contains over 6 000 terracotta warriors with pikes (as long as three meters), dagger-axes, and halberds in their hands. In the middle of the two arrays stand 38 columns of terracotta warriors, all facing east. Between each pair of columns are one or two chariots, behind which are three armored warriors. Pit 2 is about 6 000 square meters in area, and is in the shape of a triangle. The terracotta warriors arrayed in this pit are mixed military forces, including archers, chariots, and horsemen. On the east end of the pit is an infantry square. On the south end, 64 war chariots make a combat formation, and there also stands eight rows of cavalrymen. Pit 3 is a "sunken-glyph" pit with a chariot and 68 terracotta warriors within. The total area of this pit is 520 square meters, and this is likely the command center

说起秦始皇陵，人们一定会提到兵马俑。

据说，秦始皇陵附近西杨村的村民在打水井时，不时地挖出当地人俗称的"瓦盆爷"。这让他们很生气，以为把水井打在了古庙遗址上。为了泄愤，人们便把"瓦盆爷"吊在树上，然后砸碎，或者放在太阳下暴晒，以示惩罚。来检查打井工作的人把此事上报给县文化馆，文化馆随即派人将碎片取回县里修复。1974年7月，国家文物局组织"秦始皇陵秦俑坑考古发掘队"展开发掘。经过近两年的发掘，人们在距离陵墓1.5公里处，发现了三个大型陪葬的兵马俑坑。这是一个重大的考古发现。

按照被发现的时间，这些兵马俑坑分别被命名为一、二、三号坑，这三个坑的总面积达22 780平方米。一号坑是长方形的军事方阵，东西长230米，宽62米，深5米，总面积14 260平方米。俑坑的东面排列着三排面向东的陶制武士俑，共210个。按照真人大小制作的这些武士俑身穿战袍，神态各异，服饰装束各不相同，栩栩如生。坑的南边和北边，各有一排面向南、向北的铠甲武士俑，共6 000名。这些铠甲武士俑手执3米左右的长矛、戈、戟等兵器。中间是38列面向东的武士俑，每一纵队之中有一辆或两辆战车，每辆战车的后面有三名身着铠甲的武士俑。二号坑面积约6 000平方米，外形像一把曲尺。陈列的是一个多兵种组成的混合兵团。坑的东端是步兵方阵，南端是由64辆战车组成的车兵方阵，另外还有8队骑兵。三号坑是一个"凹"字形的俑坑，有战车一辆，陶俑68个，面积约

for the underground army.

Buried together with such a massive terracotta army in his mausoleum, Qin Shihuang is unparalleled in Chinese history. The vast number of terracotta warriors and horses represented the army of the Qin Dynasty, and the Qin people hoped that these terracotta warriors and horses could guard their emperor into another world. Qin Shihuang aspired for absolute power throughout his life, so it was only fitting that he would want to bring great power with him into the afterlife.

Scientists have all marveled at the techniques that the Qin employed to prevent the weapons from rusting in the pits where the terracotta warriors were found. Some of these weapons, such as bronze swords and dagger-axes, were actual weapons used in wars at the time of the Qin Emperor. Despite being buried for over 2 000 years, their surfaces are free of rust, and they are still sharp enough to kill. Through scientific testing, it was discovered that there is an oxide coating of chromic salt on the surface of these weapons, about 10~15 micron thick. The oxide has served as an oily film on the metal surface, thus keeping the weapons from rusting. A similar technique for preventing rust using an oxide solution of chromic salt was discovered by German scientists in the 1930s, but evidence suggests that Chinese craftsmen already employed this technique two millennia ago.

Another significant discovery was the unearthing of bronze chariots and horses 20 meters west of the mound that marks Qin Shihuang's Mausoleum. The bronze chariots and horses are exact imitations of the real chariots, horses, and drivers used by Qin Shihuang when making his journey. Each of the four-horse chariots comprises more than 3 400 parts, and each is 2.3 meters long and 1.65 meters high. The horses themselves are 0.66 meters high and 1.2 meters long. The total weight of each set of chariot, horses, and driver is 1 243 kilograms, and each set of chariot and horses is decorated with one 1 720 pieces of gold and silver. The elliptical, umbrella-like canopy of the chariot is four millimeters thick, and the windows are only one millimeter thick, with many small holes for ventilation. Qin Shihuang prepared all of these bronze chariots and horses for himself, believing that he might need them in the underground world. Their superb craftsmanship might even rival that of the great sculptures of ancient Greece or Rome.

520平方米，它可能是地下军阵的指挥部。

秦始皇陵用庞大的兵马俑部队作为陪葬品，在中国历史上绝无仅有。数量如此巨大的秦兵马俑象征着秦王朝的军队，秦人需要它们在另一个世界里护卫着秦始皇。秦始皇不仅渴望自己在人间帝国拥有绝对的权力，而且想象着把这一权力带到阴间。

秦俑坑中的兵器防锈技术一直让科学家惊叹。俑坑中的一些青铜剑、戈等兵器，都是实战兵器，它们历经两千多年表面仍没有生锈，且具有杀伤力。经科学检测，在它们的表面有一层厚约10~15微米的含铬（gè）盐氧化物的氧化层，氧化层作为防锈膜，使这些兵器不生锈。铬盐氧化物的防锈技术，在20世纪30年代由德国科学家发明，但两千多年前中国工匠的手中就已运用这一技术，实在令人惊讶。

在秦始皇陵西侧20米处出土的铜车马同样令人惊叹。铜车马是模拟秦始皇出行的车辆，车马由3 400多个零部件组装而成。车长2.3米，高1.65米；马高0.66米，身长1.2米。车、马、人总重量达1 243公斤。车马的装饰品用金银制作，共计1 720件。伞状车盖厚4毫米，车窗仅厚1毫米，且有许多小孔。铜车马是秦始皇为自己在地下王国出巡时准备的，制作工艺高超，造型艺术逼真，可与古希腊、罗马的雕塑作品比美。

阿房宫图
Picture of the Epang Palace

十一　巡游在现实与仙境中

Chapter XI　Between Reality and Daydreams

Qin Shihuang was an industrious emperor; every day he would read over large numbers of petitions to the throne. He even set a rule for himself that he would not stop to rest until he had finished 30 kilograms of petitions (written at that time on bamboo slips). As such, an inscription on tablets that date back to the Qin Dynasty notes that the emperor worked from dawn until dusk, and never slackened in his work ethic.

Qin Shihuang also spent much of his time traveling around his empire, taking five journeys across most of his territory over an 11-year period, and leaving his mark on everywhere from Longxi in the west to Jiuyuan in the north, and from Yunmeng in the south to the shore of the ocean to the east. He traveled almost the entire empire. Although the emperor could afford the travel, the tour at that time was tiring, from which we can see that Qin Shihuang was very industrious.

According to ancient protocol, rulers of the Zhou Dynasty also made inspection tours of their states, though they traveled primarily out of custom or for military purposes not out of their enthusiasm. But Qin Shihuang made a nation-wide trip, on average, every another year, and his final tour lasted more than 10 months. No other emperor in Chinese history has ever traveled as extensively as the Qin Emperor.

Qin Shihuang's motives for travel remain a mystery, although there are two theories regarding his reasons: that he wanted to see his empire with his own eyes; and that he wished to find the Immortals on the sea to attain immortality.

In spite of the hardships in journey, Qin Shihuang made five inspection tours during his reign. In these five impressive journeys, whenever reaching one destination, a stone inscription was made in his honor. One such inscription on Mount Tai reads:

Qin Shihuang is the first man to unify China, and now all in the land submit to his rule. He is early to rise and late to retire; the emperor pours his heart and soul into the governing of the state. All officials and citizens bow to his will, and all men and women keep the rituals and attend to their duties with care. The emperor's decrees will be held in honor, and will continue to be handed down to his successors

秦始皇是一位勤政的皇帝，每天都要批阅大量的奏章，并给自己规定目标：每日须看完一石（约30千克）重的文书（秦代的公文都是写在竹木简上），看不完不休息。秦人的石刻碑文中也称赞皇帝，起早贪黑地忙于工作，从不放松。

秦始皇不仅工作繁忙，而且还热衷于巡游天下。在十一年的时间里，先后五次巡游各地，游历名山大川，西到陇西，北达九原，南到云梦，东至大海之滨，足迹遍布大半个中国。即使拥有帝王的旅行条件，巡游在当时仍然是一件辛苦的事情，于此可见秦始皇勤奋的个性。

按照古代的礼仪，周朝的天子也曾巡行各诸侯国。但看起来，周天子似乎对巡游并没有什么热情，他们出于礼仪的需要或者军事上的需要而不得不这样做。但秦始皇却明显不同，平均起来，他差不多每隔一年就要游历一次，而且最后一次持续了十个月之久。这种热情与勤奋，不仅周朝的天子比不上，恐怕在后来的帝王中，也无人能够超越。

他为什么如此热衷于巡游，也许永远都是一个谜。但有两点可以推测：一是他想亲眼目睹他的帝国，亲身经历他的帝国的伟大；二是他对海上神仙的向往。

秦始皇不辞劳苦，奔波各地，五次巡游，所到之处，都刻石树碑。泰山上的碑文写道：

> 皇帝临位，作制明法，臣下修饬。二十有六年，初并天下，罔不宾服。亲巡远方黎民，登兹泰山，周览东极。从臣思迹，本原事业，祗诵功德。治道运行，诸产得宜，皆有法式。大义休明，垂于后世，顺承勿革。皇帝躬圣，既平天下，不懈于治。夙兴夜寐，建设长利，专隆教诲。训经宣达，远近毕理，咸承圣志。贵贱分明，男女礼顺，慎遵职事。昭隔内外，靡不清净，施于后嗣。

forevermore.

As one of the scant few reliable documents of the Qin Dynasty, this inscription gives an indication of the people's feelings at that time, and passes their words onto future generations. Actually, they have done it.

In the 27th year of his reign (220 B.C.), the second year after the unification of China, Qin Shihuang made his first nationwide inspection tour. He started from the city of Xianyang and traveled westward until he reached Longxi, on the western frontier of the empire, after which he returned northeast to Xianyang.

One year later, Qin Shihuang began his second inspection tour, but this time he traveled east. When he reached Mount Tai (in the present province of Shandong), he held a ceremony called "Feng-Shan Sacrifices" on the summit of the mountain and proclaimed to the world the unity of his empire and the other exploits and achievements of the new dynasty.

Despite its unremarkable height, Mount Tai is famous among Chinese landmarks. Ancient Chinese legend speaks of 72 sage-rulers who ascended the mountain to perform sacrifices to Heaven and other rituals, all called "Feng-Shan." 1 500 meters above sea level, Mount Tai appears from the ground amidst a sea of clouds, with its peak only partially visible, prompting many mystical associations between the mountain and legend. In ancient times, building an altar on Mount Tai's summit to perform ceremonies to Heaven was called "Feng," while clearing the land on the nearby Liangfu Hill to express gratitude to the Earth was called "Shan." These two ceremonies combined, or "Feng-Shan," constituted an important ritual in the ancient Chinese religion, as well as a significant political expression. Whenever a supreme ruler came to the throne, he would establish in the people's minds his relationship with Heaven and Earth via the ceremony of "Feng-Shan." By holding "Feng-Shan," the ruler would display his supremacy over the people of the land, as well as reporting to Heaven the greatness of his achievements.

In preparation for this important ceremony, Qin Shihuang built a road leading to Mount Tai's summit and set up an altar on the mountain top. When everything was ready, Qin Shihuang and his ministers and officials began the rites of the ceremony, modeled on the rites of offering sacrifices to gods or ancestors in the former Qin State. Qin Shihuang performed the ceremony to reverence Heaven, and then ordered Li Si to write for the inscription to immortalize his achievements, proclaiming the emperor's legitimate rule over the land and people. A portion of this inscription, 10 of Li Si's words, remain

化及无穷，遵奉遗诏，永承重戒。

大意是说：秦始皇统一天下，人民都很顺服。皇帝起得很早，睡得很晚，全身心地投入国家治理的工作，官员百姓都在贯彻皇帝的意志，做好自己的事情。皇帝的旨意，需要永远记住。这是一份为数不多的、可靠的秦代文献，留下了秦朝人的声音，至少是他们想要传达给后人的声音。事实上，他们做到了。

秦始皇二十七年（公元前220年），即统一中国的第二年，他就开始了第一次巡行。他从咸阳出发，向西到达西部边疆陇西，再往东北方向，最后回到咸阳。

一年后，又开始第二次巡游。秦始皇向东游历，在今山东省境内的泰山上，举行"封禅"仪式，祭祀天地神灵，宣告秦王朝的辉煌功业。

泰山，山不很高，但名气很大，传说古代有七十二位圣王登临泰山进行封禅。泰山海拔1 500米，山间云雾缭绕，峰顶若隐若现，常常引起人们神秘的联想。古代在泰山山顶设坛祭天称为"封"，在梁父山祭地称为"禅"，封禅是古代帝王对天地最隆重的祭礼，也是重大的政治活动。即位的帝王都迫切希望通过封禅仪式，取得与天地之间的关系，树立威望，展现其与天地相配的功业。

秦始皇令人开山修道，直达山顶，建祭坛，摆祭具，并参照秦国祭祀的礼仪，设计了一套典礼仪式。举行仪式的那一天，他亲率随行的大臣登上山顶，登坛祭天。在山顶，秦始皇命李斯手书刻石，歌颂秦始皇的功德，表明秦始皇统一

to this day. The emperor completed the ritual of "Feng-Shan" by sweeping the ground of Liangfu Hill after completing "Feng."

One traditional story states that when Qin Shihuang was climbing Mount Tai for the ceremony, the weather suddenly changed. Clouds gathered, and a strong wind blew against them, trapping the emperor and his people in a fierce storm. Qin Shihuang took shelter under a large pine tree by the side of the road, staying there until the storm had passed. Due to the tree's service to him, the emperor granted it a title, "Wu Dafu" *—making the tree an official in his court. A tree that many believe to be "Wu Dafu" still stands today, alive despite its purported age of over 2 000 years.

At the top of Langya Hill lies the remnants of an ancient terrace built by King Gou Jian of the Yue State during the Spring and Autumn Period. When Gou Jian was the overlord in China's central plains, he had this terrace built atop Langya Hill, allowing him to gaze over into the East Sea from a high vantage point. When Qin Shihuang arrived on one of his inspection tours, he ordered that new terrace be built atop the old one, which was named "Langya Terrace." Once again, a monument with an inscription detailing his greatness was erected by the terrace as a reminder to future people of his visit. To protect his monument, Qin Shihuang ordered 30 000 families to move and settle the area around Langya Hill, exempting them from 12 years' taxation and other imperial obligations in return.

On his return trip to Xianyang, Qin Shihuang stopped in the city of Peng (the present city of Xuzhou in Jiangsu Province). According to legend, King Yu* of ancient China had nine massive bronze Dings* made to symbolize the riches of his kingdom. From that time, those Dings have been handed down from one generation to another as a symbol of power or dynasty. King Zhao Xiang of the Qin State is said to have obtained the nine Dings after he overthrew the Zhou Dynasty, but lost one in the water while he was crossing the Sishui River*. He sent his men to search for it, but to no avail, and King Zhao Xiang had to return to his capital with only eight of the Dings. Qin Shihuang felt slighted that he as a great emperor could only possess eight of the legendary Dings, so he returned on this tour by way of the city of Peng to recover the lost Ding. He prayed for several days before he began his search, imploring the gods' aid. He then sent one thousand shipmen to dive deep into the water in search of the Ding, but none of them could find it.

So Qin Shihuang continued on his journey to the southwest. One day, when he was crossing the Yangtze River by boat, he was caught in a sudden gale near the Temple of Xiang Shan, nearly trapping him in the river. The

天下符合上天的意志。这些刻石文至今还留存十个字。随后，在梁父山扫地行"禅"礼。

秦始皇登泰山时，行至半山腰，忽然风起云飞，下起大雨。幸好路旁有一棵大松树，秦始皇急忙在树下避雨。他因此封这棵松树为"五大夫"，松树成为朝廷的官员。今天人们登泰山，还能看到这棵经历岁月沧桑的"五大夫"松。

琅琊山顶有一处古台遗迹，为春秋时期越王勾践所筑。勾践称霸中原时，曾在琅琊山筑此高台，以望东海。秦始皇命令在古台的基础上，新建琅琊台。又立石刻，歌颂秦德。并下令将别处三万户老百姓迁居到这里，作为补偿，朝廷免除他们十二年的赋税徭役。

在回来的途中，秦始皇特意来到彭城（今江苏省徐州市）。相传古代的帝王禹铸造九鼎用来象征九州万物，九鼎于是被视为权力的象征流传下来。当年秦昭襄王灭周时，取九鼎，但在行经泗水时，一鼎落入水中，无从寻找，只运回八鼎。九鼎缺少一鼎，总是遗憾，秦始皇于是取道彭城，再次寻觅当年落水之鼎。秦始皇斋戒祷告，希望有神灵相助。然而一千名水夫潜水探求，仍然一无所获。

秦始皇又向西南前行，渡长江，船到湘山祠，突然遭遇大风，几乎过不了江。湘山祠是当地人专门祭祀湘山神灵的地方，

---

* Dafu: the address for senior official in feudal China.
* King Yu: the purported founder of the Xia Dynasty in ancient China.
* Ding: a round vessel with three legs.
* the Sishui River: a river in the present Shandong Province.

Temple of Xiang Shan was the temple where the local people offered their sacrifices to the goddess of the Xiang River. But on that day, the goddess welcomed the emperor with violent winds and fierce waves. As soon as he set his feet on the river bank, Qin Shihuang asked his men who the goddess of the Xiang River was.

"She was the daughter of Yao," said the court scholar who traveled with the emperor, "and the wife of Shun, and was buried here after her death."

Both Yao and Shun were ancient Chinese kings. Legend has it that Yao had two daughters, named E Huang and Nu Ying, both of whom he married to Shun. While traveling across his lands in the south, Shun died of illness at the hill called Cangwu, and the two sisters came many miles to mourn their husband near Xiang River. They were so grieved that they shed their tears on the green bamboo shoots, staining them, for which they are now called "Bamboos of the Ladies of the Xiang." After the two sisters died, the local people buried them at the hill of Cangwu and had a temple built in their honor and worshipped them as goddesses. Because the hill was near the Xiang River, the temple was called the "Temple of Xiang Shan." After hearing this story, Qin Shihuang became indignant that these "petty goddesses" would offend him by sending a storm during his visit. He then summoned the local officials to gather 3 000 prisoners to fell all of the trees on the hill of Xiang Shan, and afterward had the hill painted reddish-brown.

Qin Shihuang made his third inspection tour in the 29th year of his reign (218 B.C.), focusing this time again on the eastern coastal areas. While passing a place called Bolangsha (at the south of the present county of Yuanyang, Henan Province), he encountered another assassination attempt.

The man who planned the assassination was Zhang Liang, a descendant from a noble family of the former Han State. Both his father and grandfather had served as prime ministers for five Han kings, and his family had enjoined a great privileges in the state, including public prestige and many servants. Since he had witnessed the conquest of his state by Qin and experienced the ruin of his family, Zhang Liang was determined to avenge these losses by killing the Qin Emperor. He spent his entire family fortune on the attempt, hiring a strongman and forging a sledgehammer that weighed 60 kilograms, and then lying in wait while Qin Shihuang was traveling in the east. One day, when Qin Shihuang's chariots were passing Bolangsha, Zhang Liang's people launched a sneak attack on the emperor by throwing the massive sledgehammer at his chariot. While the hammer did hit a chariot, that one was,

可是这位神灵却在秦始皇到来之时，掀起了狂风恶浪。一到岸上，秦始皇就问："湘君是什么神？"

随行博士回答说："湘君是尧的女儿、舜的妻子，死后葬在这里。"

尧、舜都是古代帝王。相传尧将两个女儿娥皇、女英嫁给舜，舜南巡时，病死在苍梧山，二女追寻亡夫来到湘江，悲痛不已，泪洒青竹，竹上泪痕斑斑，后世称斑竹为"湘妃竹"。当地的老百姓将舜的两位妃子葬在这里，并立祠祭祀，由此被奉为神灵。因为此山靠近湘水，故称湘山祠。秦始皇听后，勃然大怒，"这么两位小小的神灵怎么敢冒犯我？"于是命令地方官吏，调发三千名囚犯，砍伐湘山上的树木，并用红褐色涂染整座山。

第三次出游在秦始皇二十九年（公元前218年），目的地仍是东部沿海。在经过博浪沙（今河南省原阳县南）这个地方时，竟然遭遇刺客，大惊一场。

博浪沙行刺的策划者是韩国贵族张良。张良的祖父、父亲两代人担任过韩国五代君主的相国，家族地位很高。韩国被秦国攻破之前，张良家的奴仆就有三百人。张良目睹了国破家亡的悲惨一幕，立志为家、为国报仇，于是拿出所有的财产，招募刺客，一心要刺杀秦始皇。张良找到大力士，又专门铸造一个一百二十斤重的大铁锤，计划在秦始皇东游之际见机行刺。他们预先埋伏在博浪沙。当秦始皇的车辆行经此地时，他们突然袭击。一锤飞去，正好击中一辆车子，但

however, only a decoy, and the emperor remained unharmed.

But the attack frightened the emperor, and he vowed to scour the country to find the assassins' employer. His people searched for 10 days, but were never able to find the man responsible. This was in part because Zhang Liang changed his name, and then fled to Xiapi (a place south of the present county of Pi in Jiangsu Province). Years later, when Chen Sheng led the farmers' revolt to overthrow the Qin Dynasty, Zhang Liang together with several hundred of young people also joined the ranks of those who led the charge. He later joined Liu Bang and was instrumental in establishing the West Han Dynasty. After the advent of the West Han, however, he chose to disengage himself from politics and lived the remainder of his life in seclusion.

Qin Shihuang set out on his fourth inspection tour in the 32nd year of his reign (215 B.C.). His journey took him as far as Jieshi Mountain (in the northwest of the present county of Changli, Hebei Province) in the eastern coastal areas, where he left another inscription on a stone tablet. He continued on to the northern frontier areas, where he ordered Meng Tian and his troops onto a punitive expedition against the Huns. He also commanded that a wall be built along the empire's border with the Hun-inhabited lands.

Qin Shihuang made his last inspection tour in the 37th year of his reign (210 B.C.). He died of illness over the course of his journey at a place called Shaqiu (the present county of Pingxiang, Hebei Province).

Over his five inspection tours, Qin Shihuang traveled to many diverse parts of his empire. He visited the eastern coastal areas four times, including Langya (in the southwest of the present city of Qingdao, Shandong Province), a place near the sea with such breathtaking scenery that he had never seen in his homeland of Qin. An alchemist named Xu Shi and some of his colleagues once wrote a letter to the emperor, in which he stated that there were three "immortal mountains" in the sea: Penglai Mountain, Fangzhang Mountain and Yingzhou Mountain. He told the emperor that all three mountains were located in the Bohai Sea, not far from the mainland. Numerous immortals dwelt atop these mountains, with pure white birds and beasts around them, and living in grand palaces of silver and gold. The alchemist claimed that these people enjoyed immortality because they had discovered the Elixir of Life. While some emperors of previous dynasties had sent explorers into the sea in search of the Elixir of Life, none of them had managed to reach the "immortal mountains," as strong winds blew their ships aside each time. According to the alchemist, though, there was an account of an independent explorer reaching the mountains, and this man had seen the immortals and the elixir with his own eyes. Upon reading these words, Qin

那只是秦始皇的副车。

秦始皇大惊失色，盛怒之下，下令在全国范围内通缉刺客，搜索了十天，没有任何结果。张良改名换姓，逃到下邳（今江苏省邳县南）躲藏起来。当陈胜率领农民反秦时，张良聚集数百名少年也投身到反秦的浪潮中。后来张良辅佐刘邦，成为西汉的开国功臣。西汉立国后，他归隐山林。

第四次巡游在秦始皇三十二年（公元前215年）。秦始皇到达东部沿海的碣石（今河北省昌黎县西北），刻碣石门。巡行北部边疆，命蒙恬征伐匈奴，修筑长城。

秦始皇三十七年（公元前210年），秦始皇最后一次巡游天下时，病逝于沙丘（今河北省平乡县）。

秦始皇五次巡游，其中四次到达东部沿海。他来到琅琊（今山东省青岛市西南）。琅琊濒临大海，风光秀丽，生活在西部的秦始皇，从来没有领略过。这时，方士徐市等人给皇帝写信，他们说，海中有三座神山：蓬莱（péng lái）、方丈和瀛（yíng）洲，都是仙人居住之地。又说，三座神山在渤海中，离开大陆并不遥远，神山上仙人会集，山上的飞禽走兽都是白色的，仙人居住的宫殿用黄金和白银筑成，仙人有长生不老之药。前代帝王曾派人入海求仙药，可惜都没有到达那里，每次快接近的时候船都会被风吹回。但确实有人到过神山，仙人及不死之药都在那里。这些说法，引来秦始皇无限遐想。他渴望

Shihuang was riveted by the tale; he too desired to live forever and never grow old, to be one of these immortals. As a result, he spent a large sum of state funds and ordered Xu Shi to lead several thousand young men and women into the sea to search for the immortals and the Elixir of Life. He also erected Langya Terrace, and was so eager for reports of their return that he would ascend it every day to stare off into the sea, hoping that one day his miraculous elixir would arrive.

During his first few journeys, Xu Shi returned with his fleet to report that they had glimpsed the "immortal mountains," but that their ships were repelled by the strong wind. Yet after many years, his project had leeched a great deal of money from the imperial treasury, with no results. Worrying that the emperor would behead him for his lack of success, Xu Shi fabricated a story to justify their failure to gain the elixir. "The Elixir of Life is attainable," he told the emperor, "but there are many sharks among the waves that keep us from reaching the immortal mountains. If Your Majesty would send some of the empire's best archers with us, then during our next journey, they can shoot the sharks with their crossbows and allow us to pass to the mountains."

That night, Qin Shihuang had a dream in which he was fighting with a ferocious sea-god who looked like a man. The next day, he asked his court scholar to interpret his dream. "The sea-god will not appear before men," the scholar replied, "but he sends giant sharks to patrol the sea for him. Although Your Majesty reveres the gods with prayers and sacrifices, vicious beings like this sea-god should be eliminated. Once the sea-god is dead, then deities of goodness will surely come and bless your men."

In response to this interpretation, Qin Shihuang traveled to the sea in person with his men, bringing weapons with them to hunt sharks. Along their nautical journey, Qin Shihuang and his crew awaited the appearance of sharks, crossbows in hand. When their ship sailed into Zhifu (the sea area north of the present city of Yantai in Shandong Province), they found a shark, and Qin Shihuang killed the shark with his crossbow.

After the shark was dead, Qin Shihuang once again ordered Xu Shi to search for the Elixir of Life on the sea. This time, the emperor also commanded 3 000 minors of both sexes, as well as numerous craftsmen of all types to accompany the alchemist on his quest. He prepared many ships, loading them with treasures, seeds, and all manner of items to give to the immortals in tribute. Xu Shi and his party sailed away with these items, but this time he did not return. It is said that Xu Shi's fleet landed on the shores of Kyushu in southern Japan and settled there.

能够像仙人一样长生不老，于是拨出许多钱财，命令徐市等方士带领数千名男孩女孩，到海上寻求仙人仙药，并修筑琅琊台。仙人的传说以及海上的风光，吸引着他，他每日登高遥望大海，希望奇迹出现。

起初，徐市率领船队航海回来之后，都说已经看到神山，大风把船吹回来了。但连续多年没有任何收获，费用却相当惊人。他们担心遭到斥责，于是编造谎言："蓬莱的长生之药可以得到，但我们多次下海，常遇到海中大鲛鱼的阻拦，因此无法到达神山。请陛下派一批善于弓箭射击的武士一同前往，如果遇到大鲛鱼的时候，可以用连珠弩射杀。"

夜晚，秦始皇梦见自己和长得与人一样的凶恶的海神交战。第二天，秦始皇请博士占梦。博士回答："海神是看不到的，他只是派出大鲛鱼侦察。如今陛下对神灵祷告祭祀非常恭敬，然而遇到这样的恶神，还是应当除去，善神自然就会来到。"

秦始皇于是命令入海者带上捕捉大鱼的武器，又亲自手持可以连射的弓弩，等待大鲛鱼的出现。当船行到之罘（fú）（今山东省烟台市北）时，看到大鱼，秦始皇射中了它。

秦始皇再次命徐市出海，征集了三千童男童女和各种工匠，准备了很多船以及大量贡品、财物和五谷种子。但徐市这次出海，再也没有返回大陆。传说徐市的船到达日本南部的九州登陆，并在当地安家落户。

另一个为秦始皇求取仙药的方士是燕国人卢生。

秦始皇在第二次东巡时，遇到了卢生。在卢生劝说下，秦始皇派人寻找不老之药。

Another alchemist that Qin Shihuang entrusted with the quest for the Elixir of Life was Lu Sheng, a man from the former Yan State.

Lu Sheng met Qin Shihuang during the emperor's second inspection tour, and he also persuaded Qin Shihuang to fund the alchemist in a search for the Elixir of Life.

But after two years, Lu Sheng had still not found the elixir. Lu Sheng then told the emperor that if the emperor wanted the elixir found, then he needed to stay at his palace and live in seclusion, not allowing anyone to know his whereabouts. Qin Shihuang believed the alchemist, and from that time forth, he no longer called himself "Zheng;" * instead, he changed the address for himself to "Zhenren." * He gave orders that all of the palaces within 100 kilometers be connected with overhead bridges or closed roads so that no one would know the whereabouts of the emperor. In addition, he commanded, on threat of execution, that none of his personal attendants should reveal his direction, destination, or location to anyone else.

One day, Qin Shihuang came to his palace in Liangshan. He was displeased when he looked out from the top of the hill and saw Li Si, his prime minister, coming to see him, accompanied by many carriages. One of the emperor's personal attendants told Li Si of the emperor's displeasure, and Li Si responded quickly to the emperor's whim, reducing the number of carriages the next time he came to report. But when Qin Shihuang realized what Li Si had done, he was furious, as he knew that someone had told his prime minister what he had said. He questioned the attendants who were with them that day, but none of them were willing to confess that they had told Li Si. As a result, all of the attendants who had gone with him to Liangshan were executed. From that day onward, none of his servants or attendants dared to say a word to anyone about the emperor. Even when his ministers came to see the emperor to manage governmental affairs, they had to wait for the emperor before being called into the Xianyang Palace.

After several years, when Lu Sheng and the other alchemists realized that Qin Shihuang would never give up his quest for the Elixir of Life, they began to fear for their lives. Having knowingly deceived the emperor, they knew that their fraud would condemn them, so they decided to flee. Before they departed, they spread rumors to defame the character of Qin Shihuang. They said that he was a haughty and arrogant man; that because of his ascension to emperor, he believed that he was greater than all of the rulers before him; that he made ostentatious displays of his power through his harsh punishments; that he refused to listen to his ministers' advice, and they did not dare to speak

过了两年，卢生始终未能得到仙药。他认为，要想找到仙药，皇帝应隐居宫中，不让群臣知道自己的踪迹。秦始皇听信了他的话，从此不称"朕"，而改称"真人"，并命令把咸阳附近二百里之内的二百七十座宫殿之间全用高架桥式的道路和封闭道路连起来，这样其他人就不会知道皇帝的行踪。另外还规定随行人员对皇帝出行的方向、目的地和居住地点都严格保密，有泄密者，一律处死。

有一次，秦始皇来到梁山宫，从山上远远望见丞相李斯的随行车辆很多，心里很不高兴。始皇身边的侍臣将这事告诉了李斯，李斯马上就减少了随行的车辆。秦始皇注意到这个变化，大怒："这一定是身边的人泄露了我的话。"于是下令审讯当时跟随的侍从，可是没有一个人招认。秦始皇就命令将当时随行梁山宫的所有侍臣全部处死。从此以后，秦始皇到什么地方，做了什么事，说了哪些话，再没有人敢泄露半句。朝中的群臣如果要处理政务，就到咸阳宫中等待召见。

卢生等人为秦始皇求药不成，又担心骗局揭穿而被杀，于是决定逃走。他们说：秦始皇自高自大，从一个诸侯变成拥有天下的君王，以为自古以来没有人赶得上他。皇帝以重刑来显

---

* Zheng: the royal " I," used exclusively by the emperor or king to mean " I."
* Zhenren: a true/pure man. According to Daoism, a true man is a man in harmony with both Heaven and the earthly world, a man close in stature to an immortal.

bluntly; and that he desperately clung to his absolute power. Through these rumors, they built up excuses for themselves, showing how it would be improper for them to find the elixir for the emperor.

Lu Sheng and his men especaped. When Qin Shihuang heard these rumors, he was indignant. By his orders, all of the Confucian scholars and alchemists in Xianyang were thrown into prison and tortured for evidence of treason. Over 460 of these scholars and alchemists were found guilty and then buried alive, referred to in historical records as "burying the imperial scholars alive." When Fusu, Qin Shihuang's eldest son, was informed of this event, he wrote a letter to his father, in which he wrote, "We have recently achieved a stable regime, and the people in the remote areas have not yet pledged their allegiance to the Qin Dynasty. These scholars are all important intellectuals, and are learned in the respected classics of Confucianism. If we impose such a harsh punishment on them, then this will cause greater instability in our young dynasty, and I beg that Your Majesty reconsider this decision." When Qin Shihuang received the letter, however, he was infuriated by his son's words, and ordered that Fusu leave Xianyang for the northern border to work as a supervisor in Meng Tian's army.

示自己的威严，官员因为恐惧不敢直言尽忠。天下的大小事都由皇帝裁决。如此贪于权势，不能为他求取仙药。

卢生等人逃走了，可他们议论秦始皇的话却传了出去。秦始皇得知此事，十分愤怒。他下令将咸阳的儒生和方士关押起来，严加拷问。当时认定的犯罪者有四百六十多人，全部活埋。这就是史书所说的"坑儒"。秦始皇的长子扶苏知道坑杀如此多的儒生后，上书劝谏秦始皇："如今天下初定，远方的老百姓尚未完全归心秦朝，这些儒生研究孔子之学，现在加以严酷的刑罚，恐怕天下不得安宁。请陛下三思。"秦始皇大怒，下令让扶苏离开咸阳，到北方边疆蒙恬的大军中担任监军。

泰山
Mount Tai

十二　帝国的崩溃

Chapter XII　Collapse of the Empire

At the end of the Warring States Period, the chaos brought about by continuous wars was taxing on the people. They suffered from famine, poverty, and illness, and they struggled to continue their lives. After the establishment of the Qin Dynasty, Qin Shihuang's ambitious projects, large-scale emigration, and frequent inspection tours to enforce the emperor's harsh decrees only increased the people's burdens. The laws of the newly established empire were so strict that even a careless mistake could cost a man his life. In addition, the nobles of the former states had lost their wealth and positions of power, which engendered feelings of bitterness in them toward the emperor. Due to these burdensome policies and projects, revolts broke out among the populace against Qin rule, which eventually resulted in general rebellions and large-scale insurrections funded by the former nobles.

In ancient China, people believed that some natural disasters (such as floods or earthquakes) and anomalies (such as a solar eclipse, the appearance of a comet, or the growth of strange grass) were signs of political chaos and impending doom.

In the 36th year of his reign (211 B.C.), a meteorite fell in Dongjun (the area around the present Huaiyang in Henan Province). As the ancients held that the fall of a meteorite indicated future disasters, one of the people engraved on this meteorite that once Qin Shihuang died, the Qin Dynasty would immediately collapse. When Qin Shihuang heard this, he ordered his men to learn who had written these words, but none of the local people would admit to it. As a superstitious man who saw this as an ill omen of his reign, Qin Shihuang ordered that all of those who lived in the area be put to death, and that the meteorite be burned.

In the 37th year of his reign (210 B.C.), Qin Shihuang set out on his final inspection tour. This time, he traveled to the southeastern areas, as his court astrologer had recently observed an unusual haze of clouds in the southeast. It was generally believed at the time that under such a haze of clouds, an emperor would be born—and if the haze was not dissipated in time, the Qin Dynasty would face the threat of collapse and overthrow. To deal with this "geomantic omen," Qin Shihuang visited the area in person.

Qin Shihuang traveled with a large procession, including a train of attendants, as well as Li Si, his prime minister, Huhai, one of his younger sons, and Zhao Gao, his chief eunuch. When they arrived in Yunmeng, they began to travel by water, and then traveled down the Yangtze River until they reached the present day provinces of Jiangsu and Zhejiang. Over the course of his journey, Qin Shihuang heard that Jinling (the present city of Nanjing in

战国末期多年战乱，给人们带来了巨大的苦难，人民贫病穷困，维持生活已经十分困难。秦王朝建立之后，庞大的工程、大规模的迁移、帝王频繁的巡游等等，给人民造成沉重的负担。加之秦王朝法律严酷，民众稍有不慎，就会受到严厉的惩罚。统一之前的六国贵族失去原有的财富与地位，对秦王朝同样深怀仇恨。民众忍无可忍，尝试着各种反抗，最终爆发了民众的起义和贵族大规模的颠覆活动。

在中国古代，人们认为，自然界出现灾难（洪水、地震等）与异常（日食、彗星或长出奇怪的草等）的现象，是对混乱的政治局势的一种警示。

秦始皇三十六年（公元前211年），东郡（今河南省淮阳一带）落下一块大陨（yǔn）石。古人认为陨石的坠落意味着社会即将发生严重灾难。有人在陨石上刻上"始皇帝死而地分"七个字，意思是说，一旦秦始皇去世，秦王朝就会土崩瓦解。秦始皇知道后，认为很不吉利，派人追查刻字人。当地百姓无人承认，秦始皇一怒之下便命令把陨石附近的居民全部杀死，然后将陨石烧毁。

秦始皇秦始皇三十七年（公元前210年），他最后一次踏上巡游之路，方向是东南方。负责看星象的官吏在东南方向看到一种奇怪的云气，当时的人认为，在云气对应的地方将有帝王降生。如果不及时消除这股"气"，秦朝就会面临着灭亡的危险。而解决的办法，就是秦始皇亲自到那里去，破坏当地的"风水"。

秦始皇巡游的队伍十分浩大，跟随的主要成员有丞相李斯、小儿子胡亥以及宦官赵高。秦始皇先到云梦，然后又改乘大船，沿长江东下，来到了现在的江苏、浙江一带。有人说金陵（今

Jiangsu Province) was a place full of hidden dragons and crouching tigers,* so he ordered that his men dig up the hill north of the city so that he could cut off the "Dragon Vein." To debase the city, he changed its name from "Jinling" into "Moling," as "Jin" means "gold" while "Mo" means "hay," which was deemed worthless. Afterward, he continued his journey to kuaiji (in the present Zhejiang Province), where he inscribed his great achievements on yet another stone tablet. Following that, he headed north until he finally arrived at Langya Hill to search for the Elixir of Life.

Before long, Qin Shihuang fell severely ill, and he urged his men to quicken their pace and return to the capital, for fear that he might die during the journey. When they arrived to Shaqiu, Qin Shihuang knew that his death was near, and he ordered Li Si and Zhao Gao to write a letter for him to his eldest son, Fusu. In the letter, he demanded that Fusu shift the full command of the army to Meng Tian and return to Xianyang as quickly as possible so that he could preside over his funeral. But Qin Shihuang succumbed to the illness before he could send the letter.

It is ironic that Qin Shihuang should die in Shaqiu, as it was within the territory of the former Zhao State. Like falling leaves will return to their roots, Qin Shihuang was born in the Zhao State and died not far from his birthplace. He was only 50 years old.

Qin Shihuang died in a place far removed from the capital, so to prevent a wave of political turmoil, his attendants did not announce his death to the public. They continued to offer the dead emperor meals, and also asked him for his instructions. Of all of the attendants who accompanied the emperor, only Zhao Gao, Li Si, Huhai and a few other of the eunuchs knew of his death. Due to the hot weather, Zhao Gao and others worried that the rotten stench of the emperor's decaying corpse would arouse suspicion among the other attendants, so they placed 60 kilograms of abalone in the carriage to mask the decaying stench with the odor of fish. Qin Shihuang, who had been mighty and invincible throughout his life, was now rotting in his magnificent carriage with a pile of abalone.

Li Bai, the great poet in the Tang Dynasty, praised Qin Shihuang in one of his poems. He wrote:

"Born with resolve and determination,
he dominates the most brilliant
with his unparalleled capacity and might."

This is an excellent portrayal of Qin Shihuang's early life and reign. Over the course of empowering the Qin State and fighting to unify China, Qin Shihuang

江苏省南京市）是藏龙卧虎的地方，秦始皇就命人挖掘北山，从而绝断当地的王者气象，又把金陵改为秣陵，从名字上贬低它。他又来到会稽（在今浙江）这个地方，刻石颂德，炫耀自己的丰功伟业。最后，北上琅琊，寻求仙药。

后来，秦始皇一病不起，他担心死在途中，催促前行，到达沙丘的时候，他知道自己将不久于人世，便命李斯和赵高给长子扶苏写信："以兵属蒙恬，与丧会咸阳而葬。"意思是请扶苏委托蒙恬全权管理军队，尽快赶回咸阳，主办自己的葬礼。然而书信还未送出，秦始皇便病逝了。

沙丘原是赵国的故地，秦始皇生于赵国，又死于赵地，落叶归根。这一年，他五十岁。

秦始皇病逝在外，为防止引起国内动乱，随从们没有及时宣布消息。随行人员每天照样给皇帝送饭、请示。知道秦始皇去世的人只有赵高、李斯、胡亥和四五个亲信的宦官。当时天气很热，赵高等怕尸体的腐烂味传出车外，引起群臣猜疑，就在车上装了一百二十斤鲍鱼，用鲍鱼的腥味遮掩秦始皇遗体的腐臭。一世威武的秦始皇竟与鲍鱼一同腐烂。

唐代大诗人李白称秦始皇"明断自天启，大略驾群才"，这确实是秦始皇前期生涯的写照。富国强兵，统一天下，秦始皇做

---

* In China, the five-clawed dragon is always a symbol of the Chinese emperors, so people usually associate hidden dragons with people of outstanding ability　and some of these people have the potential to be kings or emperors.

made many wise decisions and enacted effective policies. However, in his later years, he made many serious errors in judgment, including his failure to effectively appoint his successor. One reason that he may not have paid much attention to matters of succession was that he did not believe he would leave his empire so soon; he dreamed of gaining the Elixir of Life, and becoming an immortal god king. On his deathbed, while he did write a letter ordering Fusu to return to Xianyang to preside over his funeral, he did not explicitly state that Fusu should be his crown heir.

Qin Shihuang's sudden death left a power vacuum in the empire, causing a brutal power struggle both inside and outside the court at Xianyang.

Zhao Gao came from a noble family of the Zhao State before the Qin unification. Due to the negative impact that unification had on his family, they were left stranded in the Qin State. His father later committed a crime and was castrated as punishment, while his mother became a maid in the court. Zhao Gao was an illegitimate child of his mother, and according to Qin law, he was also castrated, and was appointed to work in the court as a eunuch. Zhao Gao was both strong in body and knowledgeable in matters of law, which earned him the approval of the emperor. He was appointed to a high position in the court, offering him the opportunity to become one of the emperor's closest advisors. He also served as a tutor to Huhai, Qin Shihuang's youngest son, thus strengthening his ties to the emperor and his family. Even when Zhao Gao was found guilty of breaking the law, the emperor pardoned him, and allowed him to retain his position as chief eunuch.

After the emperor's death, Zhao Gao desired that Huhai take the throne. He first told Huhai of the vast difference between being the ruler and being the servant, hoping that he could convince Huhai to make a claim to the throne. But according to tradition, the crown heir should be the eldest son of the emperor. Huhai thought that dethroning the eldest son and replacing him with the younger son would be disloyal, and he also believed that contradicting his late father's edict was an act of disobedience, and that using an underhanded method to take the throne would only establish him as a man with little talent who manipulated others for his own gain. Disloyalty, disobedience, and incapacity all broke the unwritten rules of traditional ethics, for which he would not only be severely condemned by the people, but would also invite trouble for himself and endanger national stability. But Zhao Gao persisted in trying to persuade Huhai to take the throne. He told him that if he wanted to achieve great success, he should not be overcautious, and that if he paid too much attention to small matters, he would neglect the overall situation before

出许多明智的决策。但在后期，他存在着十分严重的失误。其中一个问题是没有安排好继承人。他可能没有预料到，自己竟然这么快就离开了他的帝国。他一直梦想着长生不老，期盼能够找到成为仙人的药物，弥留之际，他也仅仅是把在蒙恬军中作监军的扶苏召回咸阳主持葬礼，仍然没有明确指定扶苏作为继承人。

秦始皇的突然去世，使得帝国的权力出现一个真空。一场残酷的夺权斗争在咸阳宫廷内外上演了。

赵高原是赵国的贵族，他的祖父一辈流落到秦国，父亲因为犯罪，受到宫刑——使男性失去生育能力的刑罚，由此成为宦者，母亲就在宫中做了奴婢。赵高是其母与他人的私生子，按照秦国的法律，赵高也被处以宫刑，成为宦者在宫中服役。他力气很大，精通狱法，得到了秦始皇的赏识，被任命为中车府令。这是一个可以经常接近皇帝的官职。赵高曾向秦始皇的小儿子胡亥传授政治法律知识，两人关系密切。后来赵高犯法，被判处死刑，秦始皇欣赏赵高的才能，赦免了他，并官复原职。

赵高试图扶助胡亥登上皇位，他对胡亥说："统治别人与被别人统治，为君王与为下臣，怎么能同日而语呢？"但是按照古代的传统，皇位都是长子继承。胡亥认为废兄长立小弟，是不义，违背父亲的遗诏，是不孝，智浅才疏，却巧取豪夺，是无能，这三方面都违背传统道德，会遭到天下人的谴责，不仅会危及自身，也会给国家带来危险。赵高摇唇鼓舌，对胡亥说：做大事不应拘小节，只看到小事而看不到大局，会有祸害。

him and miss the opportunity of a lifetime. Under Zhao Gao's continued persuasion, Huhai at last agreed to make a claim to the throne.

After persuading Huhai, Zhao Gao began trying to convince Li Si to conspire with him. Since Li Si was the prime minister of the imperial government and held much of the power after the emperor's death, it was extremely important to secure his support. Upon hearing Zhao Gao's scheme, however, Li Si condemned him, and pointed out that changing the order of succession would damage the future of the Qin Empire. Li Si staunchly refused to betray Qin Shihuang, a man who had known him and appreciated his advice when he was alive. He said that as a minister he would not act against his principles. But Zhao Gao refused to relent. He said, "The emperor's eldest son Fusu is a man of fortitude and courage. He has been working in General Meng Tian's army for many years, and once he becomes emperor, he will surely promote Meng Tian to the position of prime minister. Thus you will lose your position, and misfortunes will soon befall you and your descendants." These words silenced Li Si's protests, as he realized that they were true. Finally, Li Si told Zhao Gao that he would not stop his scheme to put Huhai on the throne, lamenting that he lived in such a troubled age.

Having thus far obtained his designs, Zhao Gao falsely announced that Li Si had received an edict from Qin Shihuang which stated that Huhai was the crown prince. At the same time, he forged a letter from Qin Shihuang that ordered both Fusu and General Meng Tian to commit suicide.

Huhai, now the crown prince, led the late emperor's entourage back to Xianyang with the decaying body of Qin Shihuang, and buried his father in Lishan Mausoleum shortly thereafter. Then Huhai ascended the throne and became the Second Emperor of the Qin Dynasty, known as Qin Ershi.

Huhai chose one of his trusted followers as his messenger, and commanded him to send the forged letter to Fusu and Meng Tian as quickly as he could. When Fusu read the letter from his father, he was distraught. The letter read as follows: "I am currently busy in making inspection tours all over the country, offering sacrifice to various mountain gods in my quest for immortality, so I could not come to you in person. Fusu and Meng Tian, you are both commanders of an army of several hundred thousand soldiers with whom you have been guarding our northern borders for more than a decade. I ask you, Fusu, to evaluate your accomplishments over these years. Many soldiers have lost their lives on the borderlands, but you have not increased our land by one square inch. You have achieved nothing of value; instead, you have submitted many letters to me, in which you either blamed me for

经赵高一再鼓动，胡亥同意继承皇位。

　　说服了胡亥，赵高开始劝说李斯。李斯位居丞相，握有实权，他的态度对赵高来说至关重要。李斯听了赵高的谋划，当场指责赵高是在断送国家的前程。李斯一再表示不能辜负秦始皇的知遇之恩，不能做违背大臣原则的事情。然而赵高仍不甘心，说："长子扶苏刚毅勇敢，且长期在蒙恬军中，如果他当了皇帝，必定起用蒙恬做丞相，那时候您的地位就不保了，灾祸难免殃及子孙。"这一席话抓住李斯的弱点。李斯无可奈何，感叹自己遭遇乱世，只得听任赵高肆意妄为。

　　赵高于是谎称李斯接受了秦始皇的诏令，立胡亥为太子。同时，给长子扶苏与蒙恬一封信，令其自杀。

　　胡亥一行，载着秦始皇腐臭的尸体，长途跋涉，终于回到了咸阳，将秦始皇安葬在郦山陵墓。太子胡亥继承皇位，成为秦二世皇帝。

　　胡亥的亲信担任使者迅速将伪造的秦始皇书信送到扶苏、蒙恬的军队中。扶苏一看到书信，就流下了眼泪。书信中说："我巡行天下，祭祀各地山神，以求延长寿命。现在扶苏与将军蒙恬率领数十万大军守卫北部边疆，已经有十多年了。这十多年中，不但没有拓展边疆，反而损耗了大量的兵力。没有建立功业，反而多次上书指责我的所为。你日夜怨恨我把你遣送

problems in the empire or criticized my policies. You have nursed a bitter grudge against me for sending you to the borderlands in stead of allowing you stay in Xianyang as a crown prince. As my son, you have shown no filial obedience to your father. Therefore, I deliver to you a sword, with which you must take your own life."

Fusu was an honest and upright man, and when he finished the letter, he wept bitterly, and began to return to his room to kill himself. But Meng Tian had serious doubts about the letter's authenticity. He stopped Fusu and said, "His Majesty is gone on an inspection tour, and he has not yet decided who should be the crown prince. He has ordered me to guard the borders with an army of 300 000 men, and Your Highness to be the supervisor of the army—ours are the most important tasks in the entire country. Yet now he only sends a messenger to reprimand us on such serious matters. Is someone trying to deceive us into killing ourselves? I suggest that Your Highness ask for instructions from the emperor himself. If the emperor has confirmed his letter, then it will not be too late for you to die according to his wishes."

But Huhai's messenger insisted that Fusu should die at once. Fusu, a man of a noble soul, said to Meng Tian, "If a father wants his son to die, then that son must die. And if an emperor decrees death to his subject, the subject dare not do otherwise. It is therefore unnecessary for me to ask for further instruction." With these words, Fusu killed himself with the sword. He was only 32 years old when he died.

Fusu was a man with a noble personality, persistent loyalty, infinite filial piety, and admirable benevolence. With these virtues, he had won the trust and support of many ministers in the court, and was loved by common people. When Chen Sheng and Wu Guang led the peasants in their revolt against the Qin Dynasty, they called on them under the banner of Fusu. Even today, Fusu's grave can be found in the present day county of Suide in Shaanxi Province. Inscribed on his tombstone are the words: "Fusu, the eldest son of the emperor of Qin." 2.5 kilometers to the east of the grave there is a spring named "Sobbing Spring," and legend has it that this was the place where Fusu committed suicide. The people regard the sound of the flowing spring as Fusu's sobbing over his father's displeasure, a remembrance of his filial piety and noble spirit.

According to the forged letter from Qin Shihuang, Meng Tian was also supposed to commit suicide. But Meng Tian strongly doubted the veracity of the letter, and he refused to kill himself in the hope that the emperor would send another decree to pardon him. He believed, though uncertainly, that he

到边疆，使你不能回到咸阳当太子。扶苏身为儿子，却不孝，现在赐给你一把剑，你自己了断吧。"

忠厚老实的扶苏悲泣难抑，回到自己的房间准备自杀。蒙恬对书信颇有怀疑，他立即上前劝阻扶苏，说："皇上现在在外地巡游，没有立太子，命令我率三十万大军守卫边疆，并派公子到此地作监军，这可是天下第一重任啊。今天来了一个使者，公子就轻易自杀，怎么知道其中没有欺骗呢？请公子再请示皇帝，如果属实，那时再死也不晚呀。"

胡亥的使者再三催促，扶苏为人仁厚，对蒙恬说："父亲要儿子死，儿子不得不死，君要臣死，臣不敢不死，何必再去请示呢？"说完，取剑自杀，年仅三十二岁。

扶苏品格高尚，忠孝仁慈，得到大臣的信任和支持，百姓多称颂他的贤德。陈胜和吴广组织农民反抗秦朝，打出了扶苏的旗号，号召天下起兵。在今天的陕西省绥德县有扶苏墓，墓碑上刻着"秦长子扶苏"五个大字。坟墓以东五里，有一个呜咽泉，相传是扶苏自杀的地方。人们怀念扶苏，把泉水的流动声当做扶苏呜咽的声音。

那封伪造的秦始皇的书信中也责令蒙恬自杀，蒙恬一直怀疑书信有假，不肯自杀。他怀着一丝侥幸，希望始皇帝能够下

could escape this fate, and he was thrown into prison.

Meng Yi, Meng Tian's younger brother, was also a high-ranking official in the imperial court. Both brothers worked for the emperor, one as a military officer and another as a civil official. Meng Tian commanded troops on the battlefield, while Meng Yi acted as Qin Shihuang's right hand in the court, and was renowned for his loyalty to the state. Since Meng Yi had sentenced Zhao Gao to death when Zhao had committed his previous crime years before, Zhao Gao harbored a grudge against Meng Yi. Now that the two brothers were subjected to Zhao Gao's vengeful will, both ended up executed on false charges.

Three generations of the Meng family were loyal and devoted to the Qin Emperors, and they all made great contributions to the empire. Li Shiming, the emperor of the Tang Dynasty, once lamented that Gerneral Meng Tian suffered the most wrongful treatment in history, and was murdered on false accusations.

While Zhao Gao and his servants helped Huhai to usurp his brother's place on the throne, Huhai, or Qin Ershi, began to kill his potential enemies without restraint, hoping to establish his authority. After he had killed the Meng brothers, Qin Ershi began to murder his own brothers and sisters. Under a series of false accusations that Huhai fabricated, Qin Shihuang's 12 sons and 10 daughters were all executed.

Huhai sent his messenger to announce his sentencing of his brother Jianglu and two other brothers. The document read: "You refuse to submit yourselves to the emperor (Huhai). According to law, you shall all be put to death." Confronted with such an accusation, Prince Jianglu spoke firmly in his own defense. He said, "When we had audiences with the emperor, we never showed any signs of disobedience. While in court, we showed him every courtesy. When the emperor made inquiry about something, we all answered him properly. How can you say that we refuse to submit to the emperor? We wish to know what crime we have committed, so that we can die in peace." The messenger replied, "I'm only carrying out orders. I do not know what you have done." Upon hearing this, Jianglu looked up to the heavens, and cried out loudly three times, saying, "By the Heavens! We did not commit any crime!" All three brothers burst into tears, and then they drew their own swords and killed themselves.

When Prince Gao (Qin Shihuang's another son) witnessed the death of his brothers, he immediately thought to flee. But he was afraid that his escape would incriminate his wives, sons and daughters, and in order to protect his family, he decided to die voluntarily. He went to see Huhai with a written

一道赦免诏书。蒙恬于是就被囚禁在狱中。

蒙恬的弟弟蒙毅，是秦朝的重臣。兄弟二人一武一文，蒙恬在外带兵打仗，蒙毅在朝中出谋划策，成为秦始皇的得力助手，有忠心为国的美名。蒙毅曾判处赵高犯罪，赵高因此对蒙毅怀恨在心。在赵高的迫害下，蒙氏兄弟含冤而死。

蒙氏一家三代人对秦朝君主忠心耿耿，是秦朝的有功之臣。后来唐朝皇帝李世民说过：蒙恬是古代死得最冤枉的将军。

赵高等人不择手段使胡亥夺取皇位，秦二世为了树立自己的权威，大肆诛杀潜在的反对势力。在杀害了蒙氏兄弟之后，又把目标对准了自己的兄弟姐妹。秦始皇的十二个儿子，十个女儿，都死于胡亥捏造的罪名之下。

胡亥派使者公布公子将闾兄弟三人的罪行："你们不臣服于皇上（胡亥），按照法律，该处以死罪。"面对这样一个罪名，公子将闾申辩道："朝见的礼仪，我们未尝不服从；在朝廷中，我们也从来不敢失去礼节；皇上问话时，我们也没有说过错话，怎么能叫做不服从呢？我们想知道究竟犯了什么罪，就是死也甘心了。"使者告诉他们："我只是奉命行事，至于你们究竟犯了什么罪，我也不清楚。"将闾一听，仰天悲愤大呼："天呀！我们没有罪过呀！"兄弟三人泪流满面，一起拔剑自杀。

公子高目睹了兄弟们连连被杀的情景，萌生了逃走的念头，但害怕连累妻子儿女，为了保全家人，公子高请求为秦始

petition which said, "When our late emperor was alive, he gave me delicious food and wine whenever he saw me. Whenever I traveled, he would allow me to use one of the imperial carriages, and the clothes I wear and the horse I ride are all provided by the imperial court. But when our deceased emperor was interred, I did not choose to be buried with him. As a son, this shows a lack of filial piety, and as a subject, this shows my lack of loyalty. Without loyalty and filial piety, how can I feel worthy to live in this world? Thus I ask that I may die with our late emperor, and I beg that Your Majesty will bury me by the Lishan Mausoleum." When Huhai read the petition, he was very pleased. He and Zhao Gao granted Prince Gao's request, and gave him a large sum of money for his funeral.

Qin Shihuang once dreamed that his empire would be handed down to his offspring for thousands of generations. He could never have imagined that Huhai, Zhao Gao and those who conspired with them would shatter his dream so soon after his death. Nearly all of Qin Shihuang's children and grandchildren were killed in Huhai's attempt to secure his power. Much like his father before him, Huhai intended to do away with all who disapproved of him, but events unfolded contrary to his expectations. His actions only served to hasten the collapse of the empire.

Zhao Gao's ruthless conspiracy not only included killing Qin Shihuang's children, but also eliminating all of the men who had worked with the emperor, and those who had rendered exemplary service to the empire. After executing the prominent Meng brothers, Zhao Gao realized that Li Si was now the most serious threat to his power.

At Zhao Gao's persuasion, Huhai spent most of his time in the inner palaces, and seldom bothered himself with state affairs. Because of this, the high ministers and officials rarely had the opportunity to see the emperor in court. At that time, due to the increasing revolts against the Qin Dynasty and the increasing number of rebel soldiers gathering to resist Qin rule, the political situation continued to grow worse. Zhao Gao, however, saw the turmoil as his prime opportunity to eliminate Li Si. In order to trick Li Si into falling out of favor with Qin Ershi, Zhao Gao set a trap for him. Zhao Gao called Li Si over and told him, "The bandits and brigands in the countryside are increasing in number, but His Majesty is focusing on frivolous tasks like building the Epang Palace, and raising numerous dogs and horses as useless pets. I have tried several times to persuade him to do more about the bandit attacks, but due to my humble position in the court, my words go unheard. Yet you are prime minister—could you try and persuade him to send soldiers to

皇殉葬，自觉地选择了死亡。他说："先帝在世时，见了我就赏赐给饮食，我出门时先帝则赏赐我驾乘皇家的车辆，皇宫中供给我衣裳穿和宝马骑。先帝入葬时，我没能去陪葬，这作为儿子来说是不孝，作为下臣来讲是不忠。不忠不孝，还有什么脸面活在世上，我请求从死，希望能够陪葬在先帝的骊山陵旁，请皇上答应我的请求。"胡亥看了公子高的上书，非常高兴，立即找来赵高商议。最后，胡亥答应了公子高的请求，并赏赐十万钱用来安葬公子高。

秦始皇曾经幻想的子孙万世，却怎么也想不到就这样被胡亥、赵高等人摧残了。经过这场劫难，秦始皇的后代几乎灭绝。胡亥本想剪除异己，树立权威，但结果只能使王朝人心离散，走向覆灭。

赵高残忍的阴谋中，除了诛杀始皇帝的子女外，还有和始皇帝一起创建统一大业的功臣。蒙恬兄弟一死，李斯就成了赵高的心腹大患。

胡亥听从赵高的话，深居宫中，不问政事，大臣很久都见不到皇上。当时反秦起义军兴起，形势越来越严峻，赵高乘此设计圈套，使秦二世厌烦李斯。赵高对李斯说："关中盗贼多，皇上却忙于修建阿房宫，在宫中养了许多狗、马等无用之物。我多次想劝谏，但地位卑微，恐怕不起作用。这正是丞相的事

protect his people from these bandits?" Due to Zhao Gao's seeming sincerity and anxiety for the welfare of the state, Li Si believed him, and went to see the emperor. But not long after, he returned to Zhao Gao and said, "I have made several requests to see His Majesty, but I have not been able to see him."

But Li Si did not know that Zhao Gao had arranged for this to happen. The crafty eunuch then told him, "It is important that you, as prime minister, speak with the emperor on this issue. I will make sure to inform you His Majesty has free time to speak with you."

Zhao Gao sprung the trap by choosing a day when Qin Ershi was resting and drinking, when he would least like to be disturbed, and informing Li Si that the emperor was free to hear his counsel. Li Si then sent an envoy to make his request for an audience, but three times the envoy was rejected. Huhai was irate at being interrupted, and he told the envoy, "When I was free, he did not come, but now that I am busy, he asks to see me. Does Li Si mock me for my youth?" Not long after, Zhao Gao brought a false charge against Li Si, saying that his son, Li You, had been colluding with the bandits and brigands in the countryside against the emperor.

Huhai immediately ordered an investigation into the matter, and from that time on, he placed greater confidence and trust in Zhao Gao than in Li Si, reacting exactly according to Zhao Gao's plot.

When Li Si realized that Zhao Gao had tricked him, he felt awful and also feared for the future of the empire with the scheming eunuch pulling the strings behind the emperor's back and rebels gathering all around. So he, along with Chancellor Feng Quji and General Feng Jie, went before the emperor to give him their counsel on how to handle the peasant revolts. "While we have already sent troops to suppress the revolts," he told the emperor, "more are breaking out in the countryside every day, and our soldiers cannot stop them all. The reason that the people are revolting is because they feel that imperial taxes are too high, and are burdensome to them. Therefore, we suggest that Your Majesty suspend the construction of the Epang Palace to lighten the burden on the peasants, which we hope will cause the revolts to subside."

But Qin Ershi was enraged that they would suggest such a thing. "The man who owns the world," he said with a haughty glare, "has the right to do what he wishes with it. The most effective method of government is to strictly enforce the law, so that the people dare not cause trouble to the state. My late father, Emperor Qin Shihuang, annexed the other six states and brought peace and stability to our land, and to ensure that his exploits were remembered forever, he ordered the construction of the magnificent Epang Palace. Over

情，你为什么不去劝谏呢？"赵高的语气中带着责备和焦虑。李斯以为赵高真的关心国家社稷，便诚恳地说："我很早便想进谏皇上了，但苦于一直见不到皇上呀。"

这正中赵高的心意，他急忙说："丞相若想进谏，又有何难？等皇上一有空，我就马上来告诉你。"

有一天，赵高趁秦二世正在取乐欢宴的时候，通知李斯此时可以进谏。于是李斯请求见皇帝。使者通报了三次，说丞相求见，胡亥很不高兴，说："我闲暇时他不来，我正忙着的时候他偏来，这难道不是看我年轻，轻视我吗？"这时，赵高趁机诬陷李斯，并谎称李斯的儿子李由与盗贼串通。

胡亥立刻下令调查李由与盗贼串通的事情，对赵高也更加信任。赵高达到了罪恶的目的。

李斯知道这件事以后，十分害怕，意识到自己落入赵高的圈套。李斯于是联合右丞相冯去疾、将军冯劫一同向皇帝进言："关东群盗兴起，我们派了许多军队去镇压，仍然无法制止。盗贼如此之多就是因为徭役太多，赋税太重。我们恳请陛下停止阿房宫的修建，以减轻农民负担。"

二世听了以后，很不高兴地说："凡是拥有天下者，便应该尽己所欲。治理天下最重要的是加重刑罚，这样下面的人就不敢胡来。先帝兼并天下，四方得以安宁，建造阿房宫以显示

these last two years since I came to the throne, rebellions have arisen throughout the empire, but you have yet to take measures to stop them—instead, you advise me to halt this great project that my father started. My father favored you with high positions in his court—is this how you repay him? How can I consider you worthy to be officials in my court, when you show such disloyalty to the legacy of my father, and disregard for my own authority?" In his anger at their suggestion, Qin Ershi called his guards, and ordered Zhao Gao to arrest Li Si, Feng Quji and Feng Jie.

Being senior ministers, Feng Quji and Feng Jie regarded Huhai's order as a grave humiliation and loss of honor, and they chose to commit suicide rather than endure such disgrace. But Li Si, hoping that Huhai would change his mind, submitted a written petition to the emperor from prison. In this petition, he stated that he was innocent of the charges brought against him, and even listed seven great contributions he had made to the Qin Dynasty. But the young, arrogant emperor was not impressed, and challenged Li Si's right to submit a petition to the emperor from prison. He then sent Zhao Gao to interrogate Li Si further, to ascertain whether he was, in fact, colluding against the government.

Zhao Gao brutally interrogated and tortured Li Si, finally convicting him of colluding with rebels and conspiring against the state. After this unjust torture, Li Si was too weak to make any defense for himself in court, and the judge at his trial took his silence as a testimony against him.

As Li Si struggled toward the site of execution, bitter tears coursed down his cheeks. He turned to his son, who was also condemned to die, and said, "I long to hunt with you again, to chase the sly hares with our yellow hound. How could our lives have come to this? Is such an idyllic life impossible to return to?" Both father and son wept at the treachery that had destroyed them. In the end, Li Si and all of his family members down to the third generation were executed.

After Li Si was dead, Zhao Gao took over his position as prime minister. Now that Zhao Gao had gained power over the court, he decided all of the affairs of the empire, and Qin Ershi was now little more than a puppet emperor. Even with rebellious forces gathering like a raging storm to attack the empire, the leaders in the court paid no attention to the growing severity of the situation; they were engaged in a power struggle with one another. When Zhao Gao finally decided it was time to enact his ultimate coup d'état in the court, he still worried that some of the higher officials would fight against him if he seized power. So he decided to test the court officials with a trivial matter that

自己的功业。现在，我即位两年之间，群盗并起，你们不但没有想办法制止，反而要停止先帝想做的事。这是上不能报答先帝，下不能为我尽忠。还有什么资格再做官？"于是，命赵高逮捕李斯、冯去疾、冯劫三人。

身为老臣，冯去疾和冯劫认为这是对他们人格的极大侮辱，愤然自杀。李斯盼望胡亥能够回心转意，在狱中上书，声明自己清白，并列举自己为秦朝立下的七大功绩。然而，结果适得其反，胡亥说："囚徒怎么还有上书的资格呢？"令赵高严加审讯李斯。

赵高给李斯定下"通盗谋反"的罪名，对李斯施行各种酷刑，李斯实在无力为自己申辩，法官当做默认。

李斯走向刑场，老泪横流，回头对一同临刑的儿子说："我想跟你一起，再牵着黄狗去追逐狡兔，还能够吗？"父子抱头痛哭。李斯被杀，全家老少都被处以死刑，夷灭三族。

李斯被除掉以后，赵高做了丞相，独掌朝政。朝中事无大小，都由赵高决定。秦二世的朝廷实际上成了赵高的天下。此时天下已是风起云涌，各地的反抗运动不断兴起，但是朝中决策者却熟视无睹，仍然醉心于权力的争斗。赵高见时机已到，打算叛乱，但他担心可能仍有大臣不服，于是决定进行一场荒

seemed ridiculous to the uninformed.

One day, Zhao Gao came to court with a stag which he intended to present to Qin Ershi as a gift. When all of the ministers and officials were present, Zhao Gao pointed at the stag and said to Qin Ershi, "Your Majesty, here is a rare horse I wish to present you. How do you like it?"

Huhai laughed and said, " Prime Minister, you must be mistaken. Why are you calling a stag a horse?"

"Your Majesty," Zhao Gao replied, "it is indeed an excellent horse."

Huhai turned to the ministers and officials present. "Is it a horse or a stag?" he asked.

The court leaders did not know that Zhao Gao had set the trap to gauge their reactions. Some of them kept silent, and some aligned with Zhao Gao by saying that the stag was a horse. But others, upright and honest and willing to disagree with Zhao Gao, said it was indeed a stag.

Seeing who had stood with him and who had told the truth, Zhao Gao set about secretly murdering those officials who had called the stag a stag. From that time forth, all of the ministers and officials in court feared the chief eunuch's power and influence. This is the famous story of "Calling a Stag a Horse."

Zhao Gao seldom reported to Qin Ershi the truth about the revolts across the country, and even turned a deaf ear to the requests for reinforcements from the generals who were fighting on the battlefront. Instead, he heaped blame upon them, criticizing them as incompetent. In the decisive battle with Xiang Yu* in Julu (the present county of Pingxiang in Hebei Province), the Qin army suffered severe losses of more than 300 000 soldiers, and was soundly defeated. As Xiang Yu's troops began to approach the imperial capital of Xianyang, Qin Shihuang's empire was falling apart from the inside as well as the outside.

From the time he had become emperor, Qin Ershi indulged himself in hunting and merry-making. One day, a man trespassed upon the imperial hunting grounds, and Qin Ershi accidentally shot and killed him. When Zhao Gao heard about this, he said to Huhai, "It is taboo for the emperor to shoot an innocent man—an emperor guilty of this mistake would lose the blessings of the gods, and may even bring down disaster upon him. I advise that Your Majesty stay away from the imperial court and remain in the inner palaces to find a way to remedy your mistake." That night, Huhai dreamt that he came across a white tiger while traveling in his horse-drawn carriage, and that the tiger killed the horse on the outermost left of the team. The dream frightened

诞的"考验"。

一天，赵高牵着一头鹿上朝，准备献给秦二世。等到大臣到齐之后，赵高当着群臣的面，指着鹿对二世说："陛下，这是我特意献给您的宝马，您看如何？"

胡亥笑笑说："丞相是不是糊涂了，把鹿说成是马。"

赵高回答说："陛下，这的确是一匹好马。"

胡亥问在场的大臣："这到底是马还是鹿？"

大臣们不知道赵高在耍（shuǎ）什么花样。一些人保持沉默，一些人顺从赵高，说是马，也有一些耿直的大臣，说是鹿。

说鹿的大臣都被赵高暗中迫害致死。从此以后，朝中没有一个大臣不惧怕赵高的权势。这就是"指鹿为马"的故事。

赵高多次对秦二世隐瞒百姓反抗的实情，即使前线将领请求支援，他也置之不理，反而责怪将领无能。与项羽在巨鹿（今河北省平乡县）一场大战，秦军大败，损兵三十多万。项羽的大军逼近咸阳，秦始皇创立的大秦帝国，此时已经分崩离析。

秦二世整日打猎玩乐，有一次误射闯入上林苑的人，赵高听说后，对胡亥讲："射杀无辜的人，这是皇上的大禁。鬼神将不会保佑，上天也将降临灾难。皇上应该远离皇宫以求补救。"恰在此时，胡亥做了一个梦，梦中他驾车出行，遇到一只白虎，咬死了最左边的那匹马。他心中很是惊恐，于是询问

---

* Xiang Yu: one of the most prominent generals in Chinese history, a descendant of a noble family of the former Chu State. He was a skilled military leader, as it took him only a few years to overthrow the Qin Dynasty, but he was poor at diplomacy, management, and administrative affairs. This led to his failure during his struggle with Liu Bang over leadership in China after the fall of the Qin Dynasty.

him, and he asked one of his officials, a dream interpreter, to tell him its meaning. The official said, "This symbolizes the disfavor of the river-god in the Jingshui River." Qin Ershi at once left his palace in Xianyang for the Wangyi Palace, which was situated by the south bank of the Jingshui River. He then offered sacrifice to the river-god by drowning four white horses in the river, and then Huhai settled himself in the Wangyi Palace.

During the time he lived in the Wangyi Palace, envoys came to Huhai again and again, all reporting about the uprisings and rebellions among the people. Huhai was shocked and enraged about this, and ordered that Zhao Gao come to see him. In the chief eunuch's mind, Huhai was now nothing more than an obstacle in his way to obtaining power over the empire. Therefore, Zhao Gao conspired with Yan Le, his son-in-law, and Zhao Cheng, his younger brother, to remove this obstacle. He said, "His Majesty has never taken our advice in dealing with these rebellions, and now wants to blame our family, the Zhao family, for the empire's desperate situation. In order to deal with the situation, I will have Prince Ziying crowned as the new emperor. Prince Ziying is benevolent, simple, and humble, and is well-loved by people, and he can stop these rebellions that the emperor was powerless to suppress."

So Zhao Cheng began to spread the rumor that rebels were breaking into the Wangyi Palace, and then gave orders that Yan Le take a troop of soldiers to arrest the rebels. Yan Le led a group of more than 1 000 men and marched to the Wangyi Palace. As soon as he arrived, Yan Le arrested the captain of the guard and said, "Rebels are breaking into the palace—why have you done nothing to stop them?" "We have guards everywhere around the palace," the officer argued. "How could these rebels break in?" But Yan Le did not listen to his explanation and ordered his men to behead the captain. Then he and his soldiers broke into the palace and shot arrows at anyone in sight, shocking the palace's eunuchs and guards with their attack. Between the shouting and screaming of those inside the palace, and the confusion and chaos of those trying to escape, several dozen people were killed.

When Zhao Cheng and Yan Le neared the place where Huhai was living, they presented themselves before the emperor with a hail of arrows. This frightened the emperor, and he shouted for his attendants to tell him what was happening. All of them fled, however, except for one eunuch who stayed by his side. Qin Ershi asked the man, "Why did you not tell me of this conspiracy? If you had, then I could have done something about it." The eunuch answered, "The only reason I yet live is because I dared not speak. If I dared utter a single word earlier, then I would have been killed before I arrived here.

占梦的官员。官员回答说："这是泾水的神在作怪。"秦二世于是离开咸阳宫，前往泾水南岸的望夷宫，祭祀泾水，并在泾水中沉杀四匹白马。随后，胡亥就住在望夷宫。

胡亥在望夷宫中，不断有使者报告人民叛乱、反抗的情报。胡亥十分震惊，派人责问赵高。此时的赵高感到胡亥已成为自己专权的障碍，于是他与自己的女婿阎乐、弟弟赵成密谋说："皇上不听劝谏，如今国家形势危急，却想把祸患归罪于我们赵家。我准备拥立公子子婴为皇上，子婴仁义简朴，百姓都爱戴他。"

于是赵成在望夷宫散布谣言说有贼闯入，并令阎乐率兵捕贼。阎乐率一千多人急奔望夷宫，并将防守官员捆绑起来，厉声质问："有贼闯入宫中，为何不制止？"守卫官员小心翼翼地说："周围都有兵卒防守，哪里会有贼人闯入？"阎乐不听辩解，下令将他斩首，直扑宫中，乱箭射杀。宫中的护卫与宦官乱作一团，或是奔逃，或是搏斗，死者数十人。

赵成、阎乐等人冲入胡亥住处，乱箭并射，胡亥大惊，急呼左右，左右皆惶恐不敢上前，只有一个宦官没有逃走，跟着秦二世，秦二世大声质问："你怎么不早点告诉我？以至于成了这个样子。"宦官说："我没敢说话，才没有被杀。倘若我说一句话，早已经被诛杀了，怎么还能到这里呢。"

Soon Yan Le and his soldiers stood before Qin Ershi, and Yan Le denounced him as an incompetent emperor. "You have done nothing but indulge yourself in extravagance and debauchery," Yan said, "and your poor management of state affairs has killed many innocents. The people across the empire have all forsaken you. Now there is only one thing left for you to do." Yan Le meant that Huhai's only option was suicide to prevent further disgrace, but the young emperor refused to relinquish his throne, and he still foolishly placed his trust in Zhao Gao. "Where is the prime minister?" he asked. "I would like to see him." But Yan Le refused to let him see Zhao Gao.

Huhai was not known for his forceful personality, nor his mental sharpness, so he began to bargain with Yan Le to save his life, "Very well. I will step down from being emperor, and am willing to demote myself to a duke." But Yan Le refused him again.

So Huhai lowered his demands again. "Then allow me to be a marquis with a fief of 10 000 households." But Yan Le refused him once more.

Huhai made yet another concession. "Would you allow me to be an ordinary man, to live together with my wife and children?"

Then Yan Le lost his patience with the sniveling emperor. "I have received a direct order from the prime minister," he shouted at Huhai. "I am to kill you, the indolent and self-indulgent emperor, for the good of all people across the empire. I have not the gall to report to the prime minister your requests." Yan Le's soldiers restrained Huhai, and the young emperor had no choice but to draw his sword and kill himself. When he died, Huhai was barely 24 years old.

After Huhai's death, Zhao Gao decided to make Ziying, the son of Huhai's elder brother, "King of the Qin State" —a reduced title from the lofty title of emperor that Qin Shihuang and his son had held. When Ziying heard the news, he feared to ascend the throne, knowing that he would only become Zhao Gao's puppet. Thus he determined to eliminate Zhao Gao.

According to tradition, Ziying should fast for five days, and then report to the royal ancestral temple for his coronation, where he would receive the royal seal and take the throne. But when all of the ministers and officials came for his coronation, Ziying refused to attend, under the pretense of illness. Zhao Gao sent for him for several times, but Ziying continued to plead illness. This left Zhao Gao with no alternative but to entreat Ziying in person to attend the coronation. But little did Zhao Gao know that Ziying had arranged for his men to lie in wait to ambush the chief eunuch when he arrived. When he met Ziying, Zhao Gao began to reproach Ziying by saying, "The most important

片刻之间，阎乐的士兵已经冲到秦二世的面前，他当面指斥胡亥的罪过："你骄奢淫逸，诛杀无辜，天下人都已经背叛你了，你自行打算吧！"示意胡亥自杀。此时的胡亥还天真地把希望寄托在赵高身上："丞相在哪里，我请求见他一面。"阎乐说："不行！"

昏愦的胡亥开始讨价还价："我愿意做一个郡王。"得到的回答仍是"不行"。

胡亥又退一步说："愿为一个万户侯。"阎乐依然不答应。

胡亥再退一步说："愿与妻子儿女做普通老百姓，享受秦公子的待遇。"

阎乐不愿再与他纠缠下去，大声喝道："我是奉了丞相的命令，为天下人诛杀昏君，你说得再多，我也不敢上报。"说着，指使士兵逼迫胡亥。无奈之下，胡亥拔剑自杀，死时不到二十四岁。

胡亥死后，赵高改立胡亥哥哥的儿子子婴为秦王。子婴听到消息后，并没有因继承王位而高兴，他担心自己将成为赵高的傀儡（kuǐ lěi），于是决定铲除赵高。

子婴斋戒五日后，将到宗庙里举行仪式，接受王玺，继承王位。举行继位典礼之时，群臣都到齐了，子婴却声称病了，不能前往。赵高一连几次派人去请，子婴仍然不来，赵高只得亲自去请，但不知子婴的斋宫中已经布置好埋伏。赵高见到子婴，责备道："宗庙大事，你为何不去？"子婴并不回答，令

ceremony of your life is being held in your ancestral temple. Why do you refuse to attend it?" Ziying did not answer him, and instead ordered Han Tan, his eunuch, to stab Zhao Gao to death with sword. After Zhao Gao was dead, Ziying came to the coronation ceremony and announced before all of the court charges condemning Zhao Gao, and ordered that the chief eunuch and all of his family, down to the third generation, should be executed. Having done this, Ziying made the ceremonial sacrifices to his ancestors and officially took the throne of the Qin Empire.

But by this point, the growing revolts against the Qin government had spread across the land, and now the dynasty's collapse was inevitable. In 206 B.C., Liu Bang and his army captured Xianyang, and Ziying, after only 46 days as king, surrendered himself to Liu Bang. Soon afterward, Xiang Yu captured Hanguguan Pass, and after looting the treasures of the Xianyang Palace, burned the palace to the ground.

Only 15 years after its establishment, the Qin Empire, despite its unprecedented power, crumbled to dust under a wave of insurrections led by disgruntled farmers and the descendants of the ruling houses from the former six states. The only remnants we have of this grand empire today are ruins of tile and brick, and numerous bleak graves that dot the landscape.

After 50 years of trudging through the journey of his life, Qin Shihuang died, and his empire collapsed behind him.

Qin Shihuang was wise and sober-minded, and possessed exemplary talent and a bold vision. Yet at the same time, he was obstinate, stubborn, cruel, and lacked any vestiges of mercy or kindness. With a grand vision for his political system, he designed a powerful, united empire, but he failed to contemplate the pale, wan faces of the common people who suffered under his harsh, arrogant rule.

In comparison with other dynasties that spanned several centuries, the Qin Dynasty's rule was fleeting and evanescent. Yet compared to other rulers in Chinese history, Qin Shihuang's accomplishments are legendary. This paradox only increases the dramatic impact of his life and reign. In only a short period of time, a small state in the remote west became the overlord of all the other states, annexing them into a unified empire, and then established an ingenious system of centralized government that led the empire into a time of great prosperity. Even so, it was not long before this great empire weakened, and suffered complete collapse after only a few short rebellions. As the time of its establishment, prosperity, and collapse only spans a few decades, the Qin Empire shows the typical cycle of a powerful regime in a rapid, dramatic

宦官韩谈拔剑刺杀赵高。子婴当着群臣的面宣布赵高的罪行，同时灭了赵高三族。子婴祭祀了宗庙，登上王位。

然而，此时反秦运动的势力已经壮大，秦朝灭亡之势不可逆转。公元前206年，刘邦率兵攻入秦帝国的首都咸阳，当了四十六天秦王的子婴投降刘邦。不多久，项羽入函谷关，他将咸阳宫中的宝物、美女抢劫一空，然后放火焚烧。

空前强大的秦帝国，仅仅维持了十五年，就在众多的反抗势力的进攻下，彻底覆灭了。庞大的帝国，留下了一片瓦砾废墟和几处荒冢。

秦始皇走完了他五十年的生涯。

他智慧、冷静，气魄宏大，具有雄才大略；他刚愎自用，暴烈残忍，缺少仁慈与温情。他具有政治想象力，设计了一个庞大的帝国，但他似乎来不及俯下身子看一看周围无数个憔悴不堪的百姓。

与其他具有数百年历史的王朝相比，秦朝实在太短了；与绝大多数统治者相比，秦始皇所做的事情实在太多了。这使得历史具有某种戏剧性：一个西部偏僻的小国，很快成为战国时代的霸主；七国混战，秦国吞并其他六国，建立了统一的帝国；创造性地实施了许多改革措施，使王朝走向鼎盛。可是，它很快又显出了虚弱与病容，在一系列看起来并不算太猛烈的打击之下，整个帝国轰然倒塌。从兴起到强盛，从顶峰到衰败，其间只有几十年。我们可以很容易地画出整个帝国兴衰的曲线，

fashion. While the empire rose to unprecedented heights of power, and accomplished projects that previous rulers could never have dreamed of, the burdens that it placed upon the people were equally extreme, paving the way for its eventual downfall.

The Qin Dynasty only lasted as a unified empire for 15 years, but despite its brevity, it created a complete model of government institutions and laid the foundation for the future development of Chinese civilization. Elements of Qin Shihuang's political system and standardizing reforms have been retained to varying degrees throughout history, and have greatly impacted the Chinese people for thousands of years. As the emperor who established many of the precedents of modern Chinese culture and society, Qin Shihuang is worthy of our continued study and attention even today.

可以清楚地看到其中勃发的力量、智慧的创造和勤奋的建设，也可以看到它的痛苦、矛盾和悲哀。

　　秦帝国统一的政权虽然仅维持了十五年，但它在短暂的时间里创造的一整套国家体制与文明体系，奠定了中国文明的根基。秦始皇所制定的各项政治制度和改革措施，其中的元素又以各种变化形式在历史上保留了下来，对后代产生了深远的影响。作为一位独特的帝王，秦始皇值得我们关注。

图书在版编目(CIP)数据

　　秦始皇:汉英对照/童强,李喜燕著:王正文译.
—南京:南京大学出版社,2010.3
　　(中国思想家评传简明读本)
　　ISBN 978-7-305-06608-5

　　Ⅰ.秦… Ⅱ.①童…②李…③王… Ⅲ.秦始皇(前259~
前210)—评传—汉、英 Ⅳ.K827=33

　　中国版本图书馆CIP数据核字(2009)第239808号

出 版 者　南京大学出版社
社　　　址　南京汉口路22号　邮　编　210093
网　　　址　http://www.NjupCo.com
出 版 人　左　健

丛 书 名　《中国思想家评传》简明读本(中英文版)
书　　　名　秦始皇
著　　　者　童　强　李喜燕
译　　　者　王正文
审　　　校　Eric Harrison Paul
审　　　读　金　晶
责任编辑　李海霞　王娱瑶　　　　　编辑热线　025-83685720

照　　　排　江苏凤凰制版印务中心
印　　　刷　江苏徐州新华印刷厂
开　　　本　787×1092　1/16　印张　13.5　字数　263千
版　　　次　2010年3月第1版　2010年3月第1次印刷
ISBN 978-7-305-06608-5
定　　　价　32.80元

发行热线　025-83594756
电子邮箱　Press@NjupCo.com
　　　　　Sales@NjupCo.com (市场部)